TUMBLING AFTER

TUMBLING AFTER

Pedaling Like Crazy After Life Goes Downhill

A Memoir

SUSAN PARKER

Crown Publishers
New York

Published by Crown Publishers, New York, New York.
Member of the Crown Publishing Group, a division of Random House, Inc.

www.randomhouse.com

CROWN is a trademark and the Crown colophon is a registered trademark of Random House, Inc.

Printed in the United States of America

Design by Susan Maksuta

Library of Congress Cataloging-in-Publication Data
Parker, Susan.
    Tumbling after: pedaling like crazy after life goes downhill / Susan Parker.—
    1st ed.
        1. Hager, Ralph—Health.   2. Parker, Susan.   3. Quadriplegics—
    California—Biography.   4. Caregivers—California—Biography.   I. Title.
RC406.Q33 H347 2002
362.4'3'092—dc21
[B]   2001047284

ISBN 0-609-60856-8

10   9   8   7   6   5   4   3   2   1

First Edition

This book is dedicated to

Harka Bhujel, whose commitment to Ralph has kept me afloat;

to Gerald Carter, whose sense of humor has made me sane;

to Gerstine Scott, who showed me how to give of oneself;

and to Ralph Hager, whose strength and optimism are extraordinary.

I love you all.

Acknowledgments

This book would not have been possible without the help of countless people. I have been graced with many friends and supporters. I would like to thank the following for their direct influence on *Tumbling After:*

Leah Garchik, who has been my guardian angel; Lisa Pious and Sue Schleifer, who read the earliest draft; Meredith Maran, my first writing teacher; Adair Lara, my second writing teacher and the person who gave me Andy Behr's e-mail address; Andy Behr, editor extraordinaire and martini partner; Jon Carroll, for his column space and endorsements; Amy Rennert, who kept me in my place, barely; Betsy Rapoport, who walked me through the publishing process; Martin Schaaf, for coming up with a title; Karen Seashore and Ann Clizer, my Sandpoint, Idaho connection; the MacKays, for the yearly bus ride to Alamos, Mexico; Craig Lyall and Dom DiMento, my cheerleaders; my East Bay and San Francisco writing groups; the Aspen Writers Workshop and the Port Townsend's Writers Week; the Richard J. Margolis Literary Award committee; my friends at Blue Mountain Center and Headlands Center for the Arts; Edna and Dewey Parker for their love, patience, and understanding for the past fifty short years. Thank you.

•

Jack and Jill went up the hill
To fetch a pail of water.
Jack fell down
And broke his crown
And Jill came
Tumbling after.

TUMBLING
AFTER

Chapter 1

It's All Uphill from Here

THERE WAS A TIME not long ago when I loved to ride my bicycle up hills. It was my favorite activity, along with snowshoeing on a powdery slope and climbing a vertical rock wall. The same with skiing: I liked charging forward on an incline, strapped into skinny skate skis or telemark boards. I craved the adrenaline rush of pushing hard. My husband, Ralph, enjoyed the same activities, and together we played with gusto, always challenging each other. We stood on our bicycle pedals and really cranked. We hung from the ends of our fingers on big jug holds, letting our legs dangle from the naked rock face. We couldn't explain why. It just felt good.

But, unlike Ralph, I never enjoyed going downhill. It was too scary. I didn't like the out-of-control feeling that I might flip over the handlebars, crash into trees, wrap myself around telephone poles, smash into a cliff face, or become buried in an avalanche. Ralph never worried about such things.

When I skied, bicycled, ran, and climbed with friends, I was often the first up a hill or crag but always the last down. I was too cautious and timid, or maybe, I thought, I was just the smart one.

My friend Peter nicknamed me the Most Determined

Woman in the World. I got on his nerves with my uphillness. He called me the Energizer Bunny. I kept chugging along, he claimed. I had ten years on him and most of our companions, but I wouldn't quit. I had to keep moving. Ralph was the same way.

At work, I received the Whirling Dervish Award. It was custom-made for me: a certificate with a tornado sketched in the center of the paper. Around the fearsome storm, buildings, people, and animals swirled helter-skelter in the air. The tornado had eyes and a slightly manic expression. It was supposed to resemble me.

A former supervisor once recommended me to a future employer. "She's a real spark plug," he explained. "A regular firecracker." The description was meant as a compliment, but it hurt my feelings. I got the definition of spark plug and fire hydrant confused.

I think Ralph fell in love with the uphillness in me. I could keep up with him on windy passes and minor climbing peaks. But I never stayed with him on the downhill. He was always too fast. He'd wait patiently for me at the bottom of a black diamond run, at the end of a long, winding mountain road, or at the foot of a crag. He was happy when I could get to the bottom of anything.

I wasn't with him the day he had the accident that left him a C-4 quadriplegic. I was at a gym in San Francisco, working on my upper body muscles so that we could go on a big wall climb together. Maybe if I had been with Ralph, his accident wouldn't have happened. Maybe he would have slowed down to wait for me. Maybe if he had been three-quarters of an inch to the right or to the left on Claremont Avenue, his front bicycle tire would not have been pierced by a tiny sliver of glass, a sharp pebble, or an upturned thorn.

Perhaps it's the uphillness in me that is keeping me with him now: the Energizer Bunny, the Whirling Dervish, the little spark plug. It's all uphill from here. No more downhills to carve through gracefully or sail down safely; only up, up, up.

I'm good at it. Ralph is good at it, too. He's an uphill man all the way. We'll just keep at it, I suppose, until we get tired or run out of batteries and spark plugs, or a whirling dervish spins into town and carries us away.

Chapter 2

The Accident

Months after Ralph's accident, we tried to piece together what had happened. He went out on Tuesday for his regular sixty-mile training ride. As he came down the hill, off Grizzly Peak onto Claremont Avenue in Berkeley, the front tire of his Italian racing bike went flat. He went up on the embankment, riding on the rim, then lost control, took a header over the front handlebars, landed on his back, and snapped his neck.

He lay in the middle of the road, drifting in and out of consciousness. We learned later that a motorist had come by, called 911, and summoned an ambulance. We didn't know how long he lay there or how long it took for the ambulance to get to him. We didn't know how the paramedics knew who he was and where he resided in order to call our home and inform my brother John, who lived with us, that he was being hauled off to the hospital. We just knew it was an accident that changed our lives forever, and it was over and done with. I didn't like thinking about it.

ം‰൙

Before Ralph's accident, I'd seen a few things. I'd glimpsed a dead man lying on the side of the road near the High Street onramp to the Nimitz freeway. I'd been in Africa, where knife-wielding Kenyans stared me in the eye and dared me to come closer. I'd slept with chickens, pigs, rats, and a crazy Dutchman in Northern Thailand. I rescued myself from a landslide in Nepal; climbed Mount Rainier; spent an hour in a gay leather bar in San Francisco in 1978. But nothing had prepared me for that first night in Highland General Hospital, on April 27, 1994, when the paramedics had dropped off Ralph, barely breathing, with almost no heartbeat and little chance of surviving.

It was John who'd called me at the gym, to tell me that Ralph had had a bicycle accident and was in the trauma unit at Oakland's county hospital. I could tell by the sound of his voice that something was terribly wrong. Without saying so directly, he made it clear that Ralph's life was in danger. I walked carefully to the car and drove across the Bay Bridge as if in a dream. I gripped the steering wheel hard and whispered out loud over and over again, "Hold on, Ralph, just hold on."

By the time I got to Highland, Ralph was stabilized, but I wasn't allowed to see him. I spoke to doctors, nurses, and social workers and completed all the paperwork. I called my parents in New Jersey, my brother at home, and a friend in Berkeley. I sat in the chapel and tried to pray; walked around the waiting room listening to moans, screams, and conversations in Spanish. I gnawed at my fingernails, bit my lips, pulled at my hair, and stared out the dirty windows, past the armed guards, into the trash-filled parking lot.

Then they called me into the Emergency Room. A social worker held my hand as I walked down a hallway, past two gurneys occupied by handcuffed, bleeding teenagers. We went into a large, brightly lit room where Ralph lay, connected to machines by tubes in every orifice.

Orderlies dressed in green, with only their eyes showing between round caps and white masks, moved out of our way. I clenched the social worker's arm tightly and looked down at my helpless husband. Ralph opened his eyes and croaked, "Suzy." His face was covered in blood. His gray hair was matted and stuck to his forehead. Out of his mouth gushed a stream of Day-Glo yellow puke. An orderly quickly pushed a tube back into Ralph's mouth. I heard a sucking noise, and someone tugged on my sweatshirt and dragged me away.

I didn't see Ralph again for hours, not until he was moved to Intensive Care and I was escorted into a waiting room by a kind security guard who told me what to do next: "Press that button over there on the wall. Wait for a voice. Tell them who you are and who you want to see. Wait till they come to the door. Then let them escort you to the patient's room. Don't leave the patient's room without an escort. When you go, don't leave any money or valuables in the room. Don't allow strangers into the patient's room. You never know who might come into Intensive Care looking for revenge."

A burly male attendant responded to my call through the intercom. Together we walked from the waiting room and through a heavy door into a different world. The hallway was wide and lined with hospital apparatus and beds. Doors on either side of us opened into rooms lit only by the glow of electronic devices. People in white—nurses, doctors, and assistants—scurried back and forth, clipboards clasped in rubber-gloved hands, stethoscopes around their necks.

My chaperon gently guided me into a dark cubicle where Ralph lay unconscious, hooked to multiple machines. I found a seat in a corner and watched the lines on the heart monitor above Ralph's bed go up and down.

Like Ralph, I did not move. It was an effort just to breathe. I tried to regulate my inhales and exhales to Ralph's loud, labored panting. The wavy lines on the machines moved rhythmically. They were mesmerizing.

"Honey, you ought to go home and get some sleep," a nurse whispered as she came into the room. "There is nothing you can do for him right now. We'll look after him. Tomorrow you will need to work on getting him out of here."

"What do you mean?" I asked, short of breath.

"Baby, if your husband lives through this, and it looks like he will, you don't want him in this hospital. Intensive Care is good, but the main ward is not for your husband. You get him to your HMO as soon as possible. This here is the county hospital and it's not for you. You'll see."

I was too exhausted to ask any more questions. I went to Ralph's bedside and kissed him on the cheek. He smelled of blood, sweat, and urine. His eyes remained closed and his breathing shallow.

The nurse called a security guard to escort me out of Intensive Care and accompany me to my car. As we walked out into the cool night air, my companion, a large man dressed in a blue uniform and smelling of strong after-shave, told me that the short distance to the parking lot was too dangerous for a woman to walk alone at night. "Be careful now," he said as he held the driver's side door open for me. "Try to get some rest. The doctors will take good care of your husband, don't worry."

I drove toward home, numb. The neighborhood streets were quiet and empty. I pulled into our driveway, let myself into the house, climbed up the staircase, and collapsed into bed. I closed my eyes and lay there, dressed in my gym clothes, not moving, not sleeping, not thinking, barely breathing.

∽◦∾

At 6 A.M., I headed back to Highland.

In the Intensive Care waiting room, three lumpy, sleeping forms clothed in Raiders jackets and baggy jeans lay on benches. They did not move when I buzzed for an escort.

This second trip down the broad corridor was faster. I knew where I was going. Ralph lay asleep in his cubicle, and the wavy lines printed out by the machines indicated that his vital organs were still functioning. I took my place in the corner and sat, as I had done the night before, without moving.

At 8 A.M., a group of doctors with clipboards entered the room. They told me Ralph might not walk again. They were giving him massive doses of steroids, which sometimes reduced swelling in the spinal cord. There were no guarantees that the steroids would work. We would have to wait and see.

A few more hours passed. For a long time, I did nothing but watch Ralph's face. Later, I called Ralph's parents, his ex-wife, his son, and his identical twin brother, Richard. No one was home. I left messages on each of their answering machines.

My older brother, who lived in Maryland, called at noon. As a salesman for medical equipment to doctors and hospitals, he understood Ralph's diagnosis better than anyone else in the family did. He asked me the results of Ralph's MRI and CAT scan. I told him I had no idea.

"Susan, listen to me. You have got to get things moving. Go out into the hallway. Find the doctors. Tell them you want to know the results of those tests and call me back."

Mechanically, I did as I was told. When I got no cooperation, I threw a tantrum. When I saw that it got a reaction, I pitched another one. I was starting to get the hang of how to ask questions and was beginning to get some answers. But they were not positive. Tests showed that the swelling in his C-4 vertebra had not gone down. In the most optimistic scenario, Ralph would have some use of his arms and fingers, but no use of his legs. I tried to imagine Ralph in a wheelchair, but doing so was impossible.

At 11 P.M., a white-coated Dr. Winston arrived at Ralph's bedside, holding a large clipboard. He shook Ralph awake.

"Mr. Hager, can you hear me?" he shouted.

"Yes," Ralph replied, as if from a long distance away.

"Mr. Hager," Dr. Winston said, looking down at his notes, "I've looked over all the test results. I'm afraid I have bad news. You are a C-4 quadriplegic. You will never walk again and you will probably have little or no use of your arms and hands. If you don't start breathing more regularly, I may have to put you on a respirator. I'm sorry I can't be of more help."

Ralph fell back to sleep. I sat in a corner in the dark. Dr. Winston asked me to follow him out in the hallway.

I supported myself against the desk of the nurse's station and tried to adjust my eyes to the bright lights. Dr. Winston looked at me without blinking; I stared back at him. "Sometimes this is as tough on the spouse as it is on the patient," he said gravely. "He will probably grow mean and nasty and take out his frustrations on you. I'm prescribing you some sedatives. Go home now and try to get some rest."

Then he turned on his heels and left. I don't remember much about the rest of the evening. I went back into Ralph's room, sat down in the dark corner, and watched the green, red, and blue lines of all the machines attached to Ralph swim up and down. I listened hard to Ralph's breathing. A man in the room next to us went into cardiac arrest and died. I could hear the commotion of the nurses and orderlies and the sounds of his wife crying.

Ralph didn't wake up again that night. My friends Annie and Peter arrived and took me home.

The next morning, I demanded a new neurologist.

AFTER TWO WEEKS IN Neurosurgery, Ralph was sent north to the Kaiser Spinal Rehabilitation Unit in Vallejo. His doctors at Highland had concluded that there was nothing they could do to relieve the contusion that was pressing against the inside of Ralph's C-4 vertebra. Ralph was permanently paralyzed below his shoulders. It was time he moved on to rehab.

While he was in Vallejo, I was taught how to catheterize him and perform the bowel program, a method of removing waste by sticking one's finger up the patient's anus. I learned how to brush and floss his teeth, clean his ears, wash his hair, and look for sores, scratches, and bruises. I learned how to dress Ralph in bed and change the sheets while he was lying on them. I learned to roll him over and rock him into an upward position.

I practiced moving his fingers and toes, hands and feet, legs and arms so that he wouldn't become stiff. I studied what meds to give him and was instructed on how to inject shots of heparin into his abdominal fat so that his blood would not clot.

The physical therapists demonstrated the proper way to slide Ralph into his wheelchair, and how to keep him straight once he got there. They had me move him onto the edge of a bathtub, but no one thought it a good idea for me to place him in it, because I wouldn't be able to get him out.

The wheelchair lady introduced me to a manual wheelchair, and we rehearsed moving Ralph up and down every twenty minutes so he would not get sores on his back and bottom. She taught me how to put on the legs and arms of the wheelchair and how to take the whole thing apart.

When the electric wheelchair finally arrived, she explained how to fill the battery with water and how to repair minor electrical problems. She showed me how to wash the seat cover and how to wrestle it back on so that the wrinkles wouldn't harm Ralph's bottom.

I learned how to maneuver a wheelchair up stairs and down curbs, and how to squeeze Ralph in and out of a car with and without a wheelchair. Someone made an appointment for me to meet with a car salesman who sold custom-designed vans for the disabled. I discovered that our insurance did not cover vans and cars and certain unique products that Ralph and I might find useful.

From the occupational therapists, I learned to assist Ralph in turning the pages of books, magazines, and newspapers. They gave me catalogs of expensive gadgets I could buy to help Ralph with the daily routines of life, but most of these items were for people with some use of their hands and feet.

The nurses taught me how to identify when Ralph had a urinary tract infection by studying the amount of sediment in his urine. We took his blood pressure and his temperature and looked for abnormal feces and bloating of the extremities. The staff explained how to recognize if Ralph became septic or got hyperdisflexia, which caused high blood pressure, skyrocketing temperatures, seizures, and eventually death.

They gave me instructions on how to use a portable commode and what to do with a Hoyer lift so that I would not hurt my back. I didn't bother to tell them that there was no room in our home for these large, bulky items. Perhaps they thought we'd buy a new house.

I attended meetings with social workers to learn how to deal with Ralph's depression and anger, and I watched movies on how people with paraplegia, spina bifida, and brain damage have sex. I was shown an inspirational video of a doctor addressing an audience of para- and quadriplegics. The doctor shouted that his disabled patients could do anything they wanted. He knew, for example, a man who couldn't walk, who went on a safari in Africa. The man hired natives to carry him through the jungle on a platform, and apparently he had a wonderful time. He didn't mention how this man paid for all the help. I wondered whether his health insurance covered it.

I met with each of Ralph's doctors and discussed the pros and cons of cutting tendons and urethras and adding pumps and special shunts to help keep Ralph alive. I talked with a neurosurgeon about operating directly on Ralph's spinal cord and an orthopedic doctor about surgery on Ralph's vertebrae. They concluded that surgery of any kind would be useless in improving Ralph's condition.

When the time came for Ralph to leave the hospital, a large, slow assistant helped me roll him out to our Honda and assisted me in squeezing Ralph's six-foot frame into the bucket seat. We tied Ralph into the interior of the car with several sheets, belts, and cords. The assistant and I folded up the wheelchair and jammed it into the trunk. I filled the backseat with pills, pads, hospital sheets, catheters, stool softeners, and expensive, specially designed straws through which Ralph had learned to drink liquids.

I backed out of the parking lot and drove onto the freeway,

heading south toward Oakland. I was careful not to make any abrupt turns that might send my sleeping husband crashing into the passenger window or toppling on top of me in the driver's seat.

When we arrived home, several friends and my brother helped me carry Ralph into the house. We placed him on the newly acquired hospital bed in the middle of our living room. Then they all said they had to leave. Ralph and I were left alone. We stared at one another. "It's good to be home," Ralph said thickly. Then he fell back asleep.

It was not until six months later that it finally dawned on me that rehab didn't have much to do with Ralph. It had been for and about me.

Chapter 4

BACK HOME

THE HOSPITAL SENT RALPH home with instructions for me to catheterize him every four hours, twenty-four hours a day. I had no time to clean, cook, or look for help.

I tried sleeping with him in his hospital bed so that we could be close. But, with Ralph in the center of the bed and the railings up so he wouldn't fall out, I was incredibly uncomfortable. I had to squeeze in beside him, my body crammed against the frigid metal bars. Some nights, because of the many prescribed narcotics he was taking, he was out cold the moment I turned off the lights. Other nights he had massive, uncontrollable spasms, which caused him much mysterious pain and discomfort.

Ralph had to sleep in the middle of the narrow bed because there was a chance his spasms could knock him onto the floor. If that happened, I would have to call the paramedics or the fire department or at least three sets of neighbors to get him back into bed. I slept with him because I thought it would comfort him, and I needed comfort too. Because of the catheterizing and the 3 A.M. pill-taking, I thought it would be easier for me than sleeping across the room on the couch.

But it wasn't. It was depressing to lie beside someone who didn't know I was there or, when he did, could do nothing but ask me to move his limbs and body so he wouldn't get bedsores from being in the same position all night. There were many nights when the catheterization didn't go as planned, and I wound up soaked in urine. It was not an easy task to change sheets when a 180-pound bundle of dead weight lay on top of them.

On the worst nights, Ralph begged me to go into the kitchen, get a butcher knife, and kill him. I would sob hysterically and whisper "No, no, no."

Once, at two o'clock in the morning, when I was trying to move Ralph, I dropped him. Since no one was living with us at the time, I couldn't get him back into the bed.

I pulled the covers off and yanked the special mattress onto the floor. Then I rolled Ralph onto it and tried to make him as comfortable as possible. I pushed the mattress, with him on it, up against the bureau, so if he had a spasm, he wouldn't pop off the side onto the hardwood floor. I gathered up pillows and put them down on the other side of the mattress. I pulled the covers over him, and squeezed beside him. It felt something like camping. I wondered if I'd ever go camping again or if I'd ever get Ralph back into bed.

Another time, in the middle of the day, Ralph's condom popped off and he urinated all over his clothes. I moved him into bed to change him and then tried to get him back into the wheelchair. But during the transfer, the bed moved away from the chair and Ralph slid to the floor. He didn't go down hard, but there was no way I could get him back into his seat. I shoved pillows underneath him and said I'd run next door and see if Tim, our neighbor, was home.

"Wait a minute," Ralph said almost cheerfully. "Turn on the TV. Move me around so I can see the screen. There's a ball game on I want to watch. I might as well enjoy it while I'm waiting here."

❧

I took a risk and removed the tube from Ralph's penis. There was a good chance he would urinate in bed, but it wouldn't be the first (or last) time. I crawled over the bars of the hospital bed and propped myself up on all fours above him.

I took off my shirt and placed each of my breasts, one at a time, in his mouth. He kissed my nipples gently. I fondled his genitals, but nothing happened. I moved my face down to below his belly button, but something about performing fellatio on a man who could not feel it, who had just had a tube removed from his urethra, who might urinate at any moment, stopped me. I moved back up his body and positioned myself above his mouth. Ralph did what he could, but his heart wasn't in it, I could tell.

I lay back down beside him, stared up at the ceiling, and wondered what would happen to us. Ralph wept silently beside me, but there was nothing I could do or say to comfort him.

It was the last time I tried to get his attention in this way. I couldn't stand his unresponsiveness or the pain I could see in his cloudy blue eyes.

❧

I went upstairs to our bedroom and stared at the bed I could no longer sleep on. Beside the nightstand was a bottle of tablets—a prescription I had been taking for the past year, but with no results. They were fertility pills. I threw them in the trash. No use taking them now, I thought. It was a subject that Ralph and I would never broach again.

Chapter 5

ONE DAY AT A TIME

A GROUP OF FRIENDS came over and built a wheelchair ramp on the south side of our house. Until the construction was completed, Ralph was trapped inside with no way out.

My parents, in New Jersey, searched for a van with a wheelchair lift. When they found a second-hand Ford Econo-line that would work for us, they had it shipped to Oakland. I promised myself that I would pay back their $10,000 investment, but I didn't know when. Ralph was collecting a reasonable pension from his twenty-five years as a physicist at Lawrence Livermore Laboratories, but I had no idea if it was enough for us to live on in our new circumstances. When Ralph had retired in November of the previous year, I had quit my job as a marketing director for an adventure travel company. We had recently visited Crested Butte, Colorado, and were making plans to move there. But Ralph's accident put an end to those dreams.

I spent my days caring for Ralph and wondering how we would survive. My brother, who had been living with us for the past two years, finished up his junior year at Hayward State University and prepared to go back east for the summer.

"Don't leave us," I begged, as he packed his bags, knowing my request was unreasonable and unfair.

"I have to go," he said quietly, looking down at his luggage. "You'll be okay. I'll be back in September."

"I don't think we'll make it," I answered, trying not to hyperventilate. "Maybe Ralph can live through this, but I don't think I can. I don't know if I want to."

John put his arms around me. "It'll be all right," he reassured me. "Take it one day at a time. One day at a time."

And then he left. The catheterizing that night didn't go so well, and once again I had to change the sheets while Ralph lay on top of them. If every day was going to be like this, I didn't want to live one day at a time, or even one more day.

∾o∾

We'd been home from rehab for three weeks when a nurse from our HMO dropped by and told me that I didn't need to catheterize Ralph every four hours. She showed me how to pull a condom catheter over Ralph's penis, how to stick the tube at the end of the leg bag into the catheter, and how to snake the tube down his thigh and calf and wrap the bag around his ankle. She demonstrated the proper way to empty it when it became full of piss so that I would not get my hands wet. Now I only had to catheterize Ralph in the mornings when I got him up and at night when he went to bed. "Get some help," she suggested. "You can't do this alone."

It was good advice, but I had no idea how to find, hire, or oversee an attendant for Ralph. I wasn't a nurse or a human resources director. "You'll need more than one person," the visiting nurse added as she left.

I was too tired and crazed to search for assistance. It took me most of the day to bathe, dress, and feed Ralph. Then it was almost time to undress him and tuck him back in for the night. I didn't know how much longer I could stay sane.

Chapter 6

OTHERWORLDLY VISITOR

ONE DAY I HEARD a loud thumping on our back door. I looked outside the window and saw Mrs. Scott, an older neighbor who rented an apartment down the street. In the past, I had often seen her walking by while I was gardening. We had exchanged pleasantries, but not much else. I knew that Mrs. Scott had lived in the neighborhood for a long time. I knew that she was under doctor's orders to exercise and lose weight. Beyond that, I didn't know anything else about her. But now she was at my back door, peering inside the window.

"Hello," I said, letting her in.

"Baby," she answered, "where is that husband of yours? I've heard he's been in an accident. Girl, I am so sorry. Let me see him now."

There was not enough room for both of us in the narrow back hallway. I led her into our kitchen, but she pushed ahead of me and went directly into the dining room where Ralph was sleeping in his wheelchair in front of the always-on television.

"Sweetheart," she said, shaking his shoulder gently, and leaning into his face. "How are you, baby? Not too good, uh? Lemme look at you. Oh Lord, I am so sorry this accident happened to you."

Ralph's cloudy blue eyes gazed up at the mammoth creature hovering above him. I could tell he was trying to focus, and I wondered if, in his drug-induced haze, he had any idea who it was standing before him. Mrs. Scott was wearing a sequined pink beret and gold rings on each of her plump, large fingers. She was positively glittering.

"Don't say nothin' now," she cautioned, propping her wooden cane against the table and patting Ralph's hands that lay flat and perfectly still on the wheelchair tray. "It's okay. You just sit quiet. Momma Scott is here and she is goin' to help you get better." She raised her head, looked up at the ceiling, and continued. "Praise the Lord, we will get by." Then she turned to me and said, "You got any Vaseline? I need some right now."

As if propelled by some otherworldly force, I went into the downstairs bathroom and returned with a jar of petroleum jelly. She opened the lid and smelled the contents, then set it down on the wheelchair tray, unbuttoned Ralph's shirt cuffs and pushed them up around his elbows. She scooped out a large mass of jelly and began to massage it into Ralph's palms and between his fingers.

"There now," she whispered, working the Vaseline into his skin. "This will soften you up and make you feel better." She turned to me again, while still holding Ralph's hands, and said, "Next time you go to the store, get me some green alcohol. It's got to be green, you hear?" Then, turning back to Ralph, she murmured, "It's okay, sweet baby. It is going to be okay." Ralph looked dazed, but he smiled. "Who are you?" he asked.

"You don't know who I am?" boomed Mrs. Scott. "Why I'm your neighbor, Mrs. Gerstine Scott. Me and Suzy have been friends for a long time, you just been too busy to know it." She chuckled. "Now don't say you didn't notice me before, big as I am, walkin' by your house. You've seen me. You just ain't feelin' well, that's all."

"Maybe so," said Ralph. "Maybe I do remember you." He squinted at the sparkling woman.

"Of course you do!" she answered. "Everybody knows Gerstine Scott. Everybody!" She continued to massage Ralph's forearms, breathing heavily from the physical exertion. "I'm done now," she announced, pulling Ralph's sleeves down and buttoning the cuffs. "I'll be back." She again patted his unmoving hands, grabbed her cane, and walked into the kitchen. She motioned for me to follow her.

"He don't look so good, baby," she whispered. Then she brought her round face close to mine and said, "And you don't look too good yourself. Get some rest. I'll be back tomorrow to check on both of you."

And then she left, her big body barely squeezing out the back door. I could hear her cane thumping down the wheelchair ramp. She turned right on to the sidewalk and headed down Dover Street.

"Who the hell was that?" asked Ralph when I returned to the dining room.

"That," I said, "was our neighbor, Mrs. Gerstine Scott, and she says she'll be back tomorrow."

Chapter 7

She's Back

Mrs. Scott did come back. She returned every day for the rest of the week, and the week after, and the week after that. She accompanied me to the store, she helped me change sheets, and she introduced us to a steady diet of fried chicken, potato salad, and bread pudding. She offered advice, whether it was asked for or not, and she gave me her opinion on everything. I became accustomed to the sound of her cane thumping up the wheelchair ramp, the burst of energy when she walked in the back door, the roar of her voice booming across the kitchen, "Get me a cup of coffee, sweetheart. What do you have to eat around here?" On the days when she was too tired to come to our house, I went down the street to her small, cramped apartment to check on her. I'd sit on the edge of her soft bed and ask if I could get her anything. Sometimes, I wanted to crawl under the sheets beside her, but I held myself back. If she rolled on top of me in her sleep, I could be killed.

We got into a routine. Mrs. Scott would call me in the morning. "What are you doin' today, baby?"

"Getting Ralph up," I always answered.

"I'll be over about ten. You get the coffee on, you hear?"

"Yes," I'd reply. "It will be ready upon your arrival."

She usually showed up midmorning, drank two cups of coffee with generous amounts of milk and sugar, toasted herself some bread, which she slathered liberally with butter and jam. When she finished, we'd discuss the rest of the day's activities.

"I got to get me to the store," she'd often say. "What time are we going?"

"I wasn't planning on going today," I'd answer.

"Say what? We've got to go to the store. We need stuff."

Sometimes we would go to Pac n' Save and sometimes we'd take Ralph to his doctor's appointments. Mrs. Scott became our constant companion. On the rare occasions she wasn't with us, we'd be asked her whereabouts. No one ever forgot Mrs. Scott, once they met her.

She was a huge help to me, not just physically but mentally, too. She was a distraction that made coping with Ralph's problems easier. Now I didn't have just Ralph to worry about. I had Mrs. Scott's needs to think of, too.

And, as time went on, our old friends faded away. It was natural that this would happen—after all, we could no longer do the things we used to do. Still, it was hard to face the reality that I was left with only one friend and that it was Mrs. Scott. But she was big, and as she was often fond of telling me, she was the only friend I really needed.

Chapter 8

FRIENDS

THERE WERE FRIENDS WHO disappeared the moment the accident happened, and friends who held on for a while but had to let go. New friends came and went, and others stuck by us. And a few old friends hung in there, even when I didn't return their calls and didn't have anything fun to talk about.

A religious friend was the last to get in touch with us. She told me if I prayed hard enough, Ralph would be cured. Then she left her husband for a co-worker and moved out of our lives completely. An old friend told me she hadn't called in a while because she was too busy buying a car. Another said everything happens for a reason. Someone else stated that God works in mysterious ways. An old buddy of Ralph's said he wanted to make dinner for us, but he had only one evening in the entire year that was free. No other night would work for him.

A co-worker compared taking care of Ralph to raising children; another likened Ralph's accident to his own orthopedic knee surgery. A friend of a friend told us of his strained back; another whined about her tennis elbow; a third was having a bad time with his golf game.

One childhood friend called from New York and suggested I

put Ralph in a nursing home where Brownies would visit at Christmas and sing carols. A cousin advised that I leave Ralph while I was still young and could possibly find someone else. Others proposed that I go away, but didn't say how or with what or where, and didn't volunteer to take care of Ralph while I was gone.

Someone implied I was codependent, like a woman with an alcoholic husband, and I should find happiness elsewhere before my life destroyed me. A member of the gym said if he were in a wheelchair, he'd want his wife to kill him. An old friend took me to breakfast and accused me of being bitter and unpleasant to be around. He demanded that I straighten up.

Ralph's brother called me selfish, self-centered, and uncaring when I stayed out late on the nights he was visiting Ralph. My mother was praying for me. My middle brother gave me money. My older brother had too many problems of his own to get involved. Relatives suggested that I move back to New Jersey with Ralph, without Ralph, with someone else—but who? My gay friends insisted I explore a relationship with a woman. Someone suggested I adopt a baby. Someone else said that was a very, very bad idea.

Many people thought I should get a dog.

∽◯∾

As my old friends departed because I wasn't "fun-loving" anymore Mrs. Scott introduced me to a new circle of friends. She presented me to Mrs. Cooper, her ninety-three-year-old cousin, who lived alone down on MacArthur Boulevard, in a house that smelled of Lysol and had a front yard full of roses and vegetables. Next door to her home were two motels owned by Indian immigrants and frequented by patrons who paid by the hour.

There were hookers, pimps, drunks, and drug addicts walking by Mrs. Cooper's collard greens all night long.

Sometimes, Mrs. Scott and I dropped groceries off at Mrs. Cooper's house. I bought them. Mrs. Scott charged Mrs. Cooper some money and kept it for herself. Mrs. Cooper was so appreciative, it made me ache just to see her.

Most days, she wore stockings rolled up to her knees, a pink fuzzy bathrobe, and a crooked black wig. On her walls hung pictures of children and grandchildren and great-grandchildren. The photographs dated from the seventies: kids with immense Afros, huge smiles, and wide collars in front of fake garden and forest backgrounds.

Mrs. Scott told me that many of Mrs. Cooper's children had turned out no good, stealing and pimping and whoring around. Some were in jail and some were in mental wards. Many of the grandkids had moved back to East Texas while others had stayed in Oakland.

Mrs. Cooper was the key to more acquaintances. Through her I met Mrs. Bueller. From Mrs. Bueller I met Miz Glady. Via Miz Glady, I met Dee Dee, her *eye*-talian friend. Dee Dee introduced me to Miz Lucky, and Miz Lucky presented me to Mrs. Jefferson.

Collectively, the ages of my new girlfriends totaled approximately 2,000 years. They all appeared 150 years older than I, but that didn't matter to them. I was the one with the car and some spare change.

I didn't know anybody's first name, except for Miz Glady and Dee Dee's. When I got together with any of them, I could barely understand their conversations. Sometimes, I suspected that they were talking about me. But I didn't care. I was grateful for their company.

Chapter 9

Help

Spending time with Mrs. Scott kept me busy, but she also provided me with the chance to search for help. While she looked after Ralph, I began to explore the possibilities of having an attendant come to our home and take care of him.

Someone recommended I check out the classified section in the East Bay *Express*, a weekly alternative newspaper published in Berkeley. Tucked between the Shared Vegetarian Households section and the Group Therapy ads, the Attendants Wanted column was the most poignant place in the paper. Each week, the helpless advertised for someone to aid in their survival. The going rate was seven dollars an hour.

Like most disabled people, our health insurance did not cover attendant care. We couldn't afford eighty-dollar-an-hour registered nurses, who were mandated by the State of California as the only individuals legally allowed to enter someone's home and place tubes in orifices. I had to go underground to find people who would work for less: immigrants and non-green card holders; people right off the boat or just out of the clink; alcoholics and drug addicts; the depressed and downtrodden; people desperate for jobs of any kind.

I ran an ad for attendant care: *Retired Physicist, recently disabled, needs help mornings and nights. Experience helpful, but not required.* The response was overwhelming. Homeless people rang us from pay phones; foreigners with no concept of English left long messages; the sisters and brothers of unemployable siblings called to make appointments for their "busy" relatives.

Ralph, Mrs. Scott, and I interviewed people who had been looking for work for years, who had never worked or barely worked or couldn't work at all. We considered the employment histories of musicians and students and wannabe screenwriters, Peruvians and Germans, Mexicans and Chinese, Filipinos and Ethiopians. The world was at our doorstep, and it wanted to know how much we would pay per hour.

Everyone had a story or a line. Anna, a parapsychic, could read our minds and knew we were skeptics. Gary believed in devil worship. Mary was a born-again Christian. Henrik was going for a Ph.D. in zydeco music. Vincent had graduated from Harvard. Candace had dropped out of Bard. Tina never finished third grade. Nathaniel was studying to be an art therapist for three- and four-year-olds. He wore flamboyant shirts and flowing pants that got caught in Ralph's wheelchair and needed to be sliced apart before we could disentangle them.

It was an interesting dilemma: how to pick the right personality to trust with the daily task of sticking one's finger up another's ass and pulling shit out onto a rubber sheet. Before the accident, I didn't know such a job existed.

✧

Brian was our first and shortest-lived live-in attendant. He lasted just three days. He was gone before he had time to take a shower. His resume had said he was working on a Ph.D. in the philosophy of religion. Ralph and I were impressed. "How could we go wrong?" we asked Mrs. Scott after interviewing him. "He's got religion."

"That don't mean nothin'," she answered.

When we hired him, Brian was living in the Tenderloin. He moved his typewriter, his books, and his small paper bag of clothes across the Bay Bridge and into our house in one bus trip. That first night, he watched me put Ralph to bed. The next day, he watched me get Ralph up. I asked him to make cheese sandwiches and a salad for lunch. I laid the ingredients out on the kitchen table. He cut four pieces of bread in quarters. Then he made eight very small sandwiches.

Brian didn't understand the concept of bite-size pieces. He made the salad by cutting two carrots in half, chopping the tomatoes into quarters, leaving the roots on the green onions. He didn't know that only rabbits eat the ends of carrots and the stems of tomatoes.

When I tried to show him how to make a salad, he became defensive. After all, he had told us he couldn't cook when we interviewed him.

"Yes," I said, "but you eat, don't you? You've eaten carrots and green onions before, haven't you? Do you eat the roots?"

Oh well, I thought, these are things that can be taught.

On the second night, Brian again watched me struggle to put Ralph to bed. He wasn't much help, and he didn't remember anything from the night before. The next morning, he watched me get Ralph out of bed.

The day wore on. Brian took a nap while I cleaned the house, did the laundry, ran to the grocery store, cooked dinner, fed Ralph, washed the dishes. Now it was time for Brian to put Ralph to bed. He didn't.

The next day, I asked Brian to leave. He was gone without a

whisper of protest. He took his typewriter, his books, and his paper bag of clothes, along with a few other things that didn't really belong to him. But he was gone, and that's what really mattered to us.

"I tried to warn you," said Mrs. Scott.

∽ℴ∾

Tattooed and puffy, Frankie arrived at our home shortly after Brian, but he didn't leave quite as fast. I threw him out of the house twice before he finally departed.

The first time, I allowed him back into our house after he pounded on the doors, stared into the windows, and whined for hours. Ralph demanded that I let him in, but I'd had it with his drinking, smoking, lying, and spilling instant coffee all over our rugs.

The second time, I threw all his belongings out after him. I tossed out his little plastic toy ducks and horses and army figurines, posters of AC/DC, half-smoked cartons of cigarettes, disgusting ashtrays, Camel cigarette pillow, jean jacket, and two black T-shirts.

But I'd neglected to lock the Honda. In the morning, he was still there, curled up asleep in the bucket seat. I could smell him, stale cigarettes and vodka, before I saw him.

When Ralph cried that I needed to be more compassionate, I helped Frankie back upstairs and into his room. The weeks dragged on. Ralph was desperate and afraid to let Frankie go. I was frantic, manic, and ready to commit homicide.

The children's welfare department came by to verify that I was chaperoning Frankie's visits with his daughter. I lied and said that I was. Then I got caught lying. Then I lied to the mediator and the ex-wife. Finally I told Ralph, "What the hell is going on here? We've got a drunk, not-too-smart loser living in the upstairs bedroom, ready to set it and us on fire at any moment! He's got to go!"

He stayed. Ralph loaned him money.

But one day, out of the blue, Frankie said he was leaving. He'd found a job taking care of an old lady. The women in that household weren't crazy like the people in ours.

Mrs. Scott and I helped him pack. We piled his measly belongings into the car and drove him to his new home. I felt sorry for the people whose house he was about to invade, but they'd find out soon enough.

Six weeks later, I found five empty vodka bottles stashed behind a hole in the wall that wasn't there before Frankie moved in. When I showed them to Mrs. Scott, she shook her head and said, "I told you so." I took the bottles out to the recycling bin for some other pathetic drunks to collect.

✂∽∽

Soon after Frankie departed, my friend Kristen learned that the man who lived next door to her, in a rented basement apartment, worked as an attendant. She lived only a few blocks away and called me the moment he told her he was planning to move and was looking for another client.

"His name is Jerry, and he likes my dog," she said enthusiastically. "And you know anyone who likes dogs, especially my dog, has got to have a big heart. I've told him about you and he's going to call."

I was more than a little interested. I knew Kristen's dog well. She was right. Anyone who liked that mutt had to have a heart of gold.

"Find out his number," I instructed Kristen. "I can't wait around for him to contact us. I'll call him today."

Chapter 10

JERRY

JERRY SEEMED A TIRED old man. Slightly overweight, squeezed into a peach-colored polyester-blend suit, he was overdressed for an interview for attendant work. The suit was out of style, and the seams strained against his round backside and groin. He had on scuffed brown boots, and he held a straw cowboy hat in his hands.

He looked apologetic, as though he'd been through a lot. Probably alcohol and drugs, I thought, but we'd interviewed worse. In the past few months, I had become a pro at sniffing out other people's flaws and deciding what we could and couldn't live with.

Ralph conducted the interview. He asked Jerry questions about his past, his present situation, and his thoughts on the future. But mostly, Ralph talked about the endless list of job duties. Jerry seemed to listen with rapt attention while I daydreamed about what life was like before the accident. The house was quiet and still. The clock on the mantle ticked back and forth, back and forth.

I was awakened from my fantasies when Ralph said, without looking at me, "Suzy, show Jerry the upstairs bedroom. Show him the kitchen and the bathroom. I think this will work out quite well."

"I do too," replied Jerry, softly.

Jerry followed me into the kitchen. I pointed out the dishwasher, the microwave, the washing machine, and the small bathroom. We went onto the back deck, and I showed him my garden and the garage.

We went into the house by the front door and climbed the staircase up to the second floor. At the landing at the top of the stairs, I paused. "Your bedroom will be this one on the left." I pointed to the room Ralph and I had shared for many years.

I walked in. The walls were lined with furniture that had been displaced by the hospital bed in our living room. Against one wall were a large sideboard and china cabinet. On the opposite side were two bureaus that once held Ralph's clothes. Now his shorts, T-shirts, bicycling gear, skiing pants, and climbing clothes were stuffed into garbage bags, stored in the attic. In the middle of the room, against the picture window, was our bed, the one we had slept in together up until the night of the accident. It was the bed I could not sleep in now. It reminded me too much of Ralph. In theory, I slept in the back room on our guest bed, but most of the time I found myself fully clothed at 3 A.M. on the living room couch.

"Jerry," I said, turning toward him, "I hope you don't mind that this room faces the street. Most of the time it's not very noisy, but once in a while you may hear cars and the Wednesday morning trash truck."

"Hey girl," he enthusiastically replied, looking out the window, hat in hand, scanning Dover Street, "this room is fine, just fine. This is where I wanna sleep. I got to always be watchin' the street. Don't put me in no back room, now. I got to be streetside. That's where I belong."

∾o∾

Jerry moved in. He didn't have much: a cardboard box full of sweaters and T-shirts; an old guitar with the strings popped; two velvet paintings, one depicting the forest and the other the desert; a bag of old tools; a small portable black-and-white television set; several shoe boxes containing items of questionable value.

His first few months in our home were quiet. He took exceptionally good care of Ralph, spent most of his days upstairs in his bedroom, watching television, sleeping, and periodically descending into the kitchen to make himself sandwiches. He packed these items as if he were going on a picnic, carrying the plastic bags and thermoses upstairs to be consumed alone to the accompaniment of the TV.

Sometimes I would see him through the crack in his bedroom door, shades drawn, sitting on the edge of the bed, watching the television with rapt attention. Other times he would be sprawled across the unmade bed, snoring and snorting, legs splayed out, not a stitch of clothing on his body save a pair of black socks rolled down at the ankles. I knew I should avert my eyes, but I always looked as I walked by.

Chapter 11

Shoes

Ralph was shopping for his first pair of shoes since the accident. Mrs. Scott and I went along because he couldn't go anywhere by himself and because we weren't sure he was capable of selecting shoes that would actually fit. How does one try on shoes when one can't feel them, when someone else has to put them on, lace them up, then unlace them, and take them off in order to try on another pair?

We didn't know what size shoe Ralph now wore. His feet were bloated from fluids pooling in his lower extremities all day while he sat in his chair. He wore several types of socks. Next to his skin, he wore nylon ambulatory stockings that covered him from toes to knee and helped with circulation, as well as protected his feet from his shoes. Over the stockings, he wore thick wool socks to keep his toes warm, even though he could not feel if his feet were cold or hot.

A pair of sandals he had been wearing had left blisters on his toes. These were not ordinary blisters. They started below the surface of his skin and worked their way out, forming oozing red sores. If we had discovered them too late, Ralph could have wound up with an infection, surgery, amputation, and even death—all because of tight shoes.

We drove to the Walk Shop, a fancy shoe store in North Berkeley. We squeezed inside. Ralph tried on numerous pairs of shoes, assisted by a patient salesman, and settled on a pair of German-made, sturdy oxfords that cost $120. I thought it was ridiculous to spend so much on footwear he would never walk in, but I kept my mouth shut. I didn't want to argue with Ralph in public, and since I knew Mrs. Scott would side with me, I didn't want to cause a scene. Buying the shoes had taken more than an hour. I was overcome with fatigue and when the purchase was finally made, I suggested we go for a cup of coffee. I needed something to recharge me.

Next door was the original Peet's Coffees and Teas, a Berkeley hangout that attracted an eclectic crowd. As we entered, I noticed a man in a wheelchair seated next to the window. Several people surrounded him. He was dressed in purple sweat pants, a purple jacket, and a purple beret. Someone was holding a cup with a straw to his lips. It was obvious he did not have the use of his arms.

I bent down and whispered to Ralph, "Why don't you go over and introduce yourself to him, while I get us some coffee?"

"I don't want to," said Ralph flatly.

By tilting his chin forward and pressing the joystick in front of his face, Ralph was able to put his wheelchair into gear and follow me to the counter. Mrs. Scott settled into the first available seat. As our order was being processed, the crowd around the man dispersed.

I went over to him. "Hello, my name is Suzy, do you mind if my husband Ralph and our friend Mrs. Scott share this table with you?"

"Of course not," he answered. "My name is Stuart. Come on over."

I went back to Ralph and suggested that he acquaint himself with Stuart.

Ralph did as I asked, bumping into tables and chairs, but eventually wedged himself between Stuart and the window seat. When Mrs. Scott and I brought our orders over to the small table, Ralph and Stuart were engaged in a lively discussion.

Mrs. Scott eyed the man suspiciously. Stuart met Mrs. Scott's stare and asked, "Momma, what is it? What are you lookin' at?"

"I ain't your momma," Mrs. Scott replied. "Don't you be callin' me that." Then, as if to divert the conversation, she burst out in song. *"If I could help somebody, as I travel along life's highway . . ."*

Everyone in the shop stood still and turned to watch Mrs. Scott. She continued to sing until her big voice filled the space and drifted out onto the quiet street. Sensitive, bearded Berkeley fathers, pushing baby carriages, moved closer to us. Hip East Bay moms in colorful Guatemalan jackets and backpacks holding OshKosh–clad toddlers smiled warmly as they sipped their cappuccinos and lattes.

Mrs. Scott went into a medley of gospel tunes. Stuart joined in and sang along with her. When they finished, the crowd clapped politely and Mrs. Scott smiled. She leaned over Stuart's wheelchair and gave him a bear hug that nearly lifted him out of his seat. "We're goin' now," she said. "Come on, Suze, let's go."

Ralph and I followed Mrs. Scott to the van. She held the back door open while I put Ralph on the lift, then raised and backed him up inside. As I strapped the wheelchair down, Mrs. Scott folded the lift into the van, slammed the back doors shut, and squeezed herself into the passenger seat.

I climbed behind the wheel and turned to Mrs. Scott. "That

was fun," I declared. "We should have Stuart over for dinner sometime."

"Don't you have that boy in your house. No tellin' what he might do," Mrs. Scott hissed.

Her response shocked me. "Mrs. Scott, why do you say that?"

"Don't you know nothin', girl? You listen to your Momma Scott. Don't you let him into your house or you'll be sorry."

But I ignored her warning. When we got home, Ralph and I made plans to invite Stuart to dinner.

A few weeks later, we discovered an angry blister on Ralph's heel. We took him to the hospital. A surgeon operated and told us to never put the $120 German shoes on Ralph's feet again. They were too small.

Chapter 12

A VISIT FROM STUART

I CALLED STUART AND asked him to come to our house for dinner. Since he couldn't drive, I had to pick him up in our van. Because he had no use of his hands, I asked Mrs. Scott to come and help with serving the meal. She agreed to feed Stuart while I fed Ralph, but she made it clear that her real purpose was to protect us from Stuart.

The following week, Stuart, Mrs. Scott, Ralph, and I sat down to supper together. We tried to make conversation. Mrs. Scott asked Stuart about his family back east, but he was vague with his answers. Ralph asked Stuart about the circumstances of the accident that had put him in a wheelchair, but his explanation was cryptic. We gathered that a bullet was still lodged in his spinal cord somewhere, but Stuart made it evident that we should not press our inquiries further.

Stuart did tell us that he was desperately in need of money. He was destitute and about to be thrown out of his apartment. He was on welfare and SDI. He had no health insurance. He could not hold a job. He claimed his live-in attendant was a schizophrenic and a drug user.

At first the evening was awkward; then it turned depressing; finally, Ralph had nothing more to say. Stuart began to rant and rave about our country's political system and the hardships of being a disabled black man in a white man's able-bodied world.

Mrs. Scott and I took the dirty dishes into the kitchen. "Girl, I told you so," she whispered. "We've got to get him out of here."

We went back into the dining room and served dessert. No one talked but Stuart. He seemed oblivious to our discomfort.

I suggested that I take Stuart home. Mrs. Scott said she would go with me. We left Ralph watching David Letterman. I loaded Stuart into the van.

We were all silent as I drove to East Oakland. I parked the van in front of Stuart's small apartment, unstrapped his wheelchair, and pulled him onto the lift, and then down to the sidewalk. Stuart asked me to walk with him to his front door and to come inside with him. He was afraid of his attendant and needed my help in rousing him. We left Mrs. Scott in the van.

A hospital bed stood in the middle of Stuart's apartment. A bookshelf and television set lined one wall. In one corner was a miniature kitchen area. A pile of dirty dishes filled the sink, and several hypodermic needles lay on a small table.

There was a picture of Martin Luther King on a desk and framed faded photographs of a young, standing, Afro-haired Stuart surrounded by other men with enormous hairdos, sunglasses, and black leather jackets.

Stuart asked me to knock on a closed door. I did so, and a voice yelled, "What do you want?"

"I'm home and I want to go to bed," answered Stuart.

There was no response. From outside I could hear the van horn's insistent blowing. It was Mrs. Scott signaling to me that she wanted to leave.

I said good-bye to Stuart and left him sitting in his wheelchair in the middle of his squalid apartment, waiting for the person behind the closed door to come out.

"Suze," Mrs. Scott scolded as I climbed into the driver's seat, "don't you ever do that again, go into a strange man's house and leave me alone in this van. No tellin' what might have happened to me out here in this driveway. This is a dangerous neighborhood."

I pulled the van slowly out onto the quiet, dark street and drove carefully over numerous speed bumps toward home. I resolved to listen more closely to Mrs. Scott's opinions of people and to pay more attention to what she said.

Chapter 13

Therapy

After Ralph's accident, I wanted to be sure we pursued every option in our quest to get him well. Insurance covered only the basic, most conservative care. Money was tight, so we did not have the resources to try anything more than once or twice.

I called in an acupuncturist, a kinesiologist, a rolfer, a chiropractor, a Swedish and shiatsu masseuse, and an acupressurist. The acupuncturist gave Ralph herbs, the kinesiologist prescribed vitamins, the acupressurist placed a smoking cigarlike object above Ralph's shoulders and waved it around. Nothing worked. Ralph sent them away after one or two visits. Someone sent over a visualist, who asked Ralph to visualize walking again.

Mrs. Scott insisted I buy a case of green alcohol, and for a week she beat Ralph's arms and legs vigorously with her strong, callused hands. She sang gospel tunes above his head and prayed. Then she brought over something that resembled a giant, vibrating dildo. She rubbed it around Ralph's neck and upper back until Ralph begged me to make her stop.

Down on Telegraph Avenue and 27th Street, the physical therapists at Easter Seals twisted and tortured Ralph into a pretzel, a donut, a big floppy rag doll. They urged me to buy Ralph a bathing suit because they were going to dunk him into the heated pool. But after they talked with his doctor, they decided it was too risky. Hot water could cause a heart attack or seizure.

We went to counseling sessions individually, therapy appointments together, group treatment meetings with other people.

I read books and articles about spinal cord injuries and talked with as many experts as I could.

When Ralph's brother connected him to the Internet, Ralph explored the Web, looking for answers.

But, after a while, I got discouraged. I'd seen movies and read stories about people who had crusaded for years to find cures, put other people in prison for doing them wrong, gotten satisfaction out of fighting for a cause. But I couldn't do it. I was just too exhausted.

I didn't tell Ralph about my lack of optimism, and for a long time he remained hopeful. He tried hard to move arms and legs, fingers and toes, but they did not budge. He stayed jovial even when bent into odd shapes that knocked the catheter out of place and caused him to urinate on his clothes. When the acupuncturist left a small, sharp needle in his neck he complained of a slight pain. I pulled it out. I cried; he laughed it off. He was an amazing patient. I was deeply grateful for his lack of self-pity. It was a quality I had not consciously known he possessed before the accident, but, evidently, it had always been there.

∽∘∾

It took me months to get therapy for myself. Everyone was so worried about keeping Ralph alive, no one noticed that I was sliding under.

But one morning, in the general practitioner's office, while waiting for Ralph to end the litany of complaints he was reciting, I flipped out.

I put my head down on the table and tried to go to sleep. Far above me, I heard Dr. Steiner asking Ralph if I was all right. Ralph said that he wasn't sure. The next thing I remember is ranting and raving about never getting enough sleep, never having any money, never going anywhere or doing anything fun. I went on and on.

Dr. Steiner looked scared. He backed out of the room and said he'd be right back. He told me not to move or go anywhere. Ralph watched me cry, but there was nothing he could do. Strapped in the wheelchair, unable to move, he couldn't get within three feet of me.

Five minutes later Dr. Steiner returned and asked if I could make a 3:30 P.M. psychiatrist appointment. I said yes.

∽◦∾

Later that day, Dr. Horowitz's office was full of shadows and subdued light. When he shut his office door, I could hear nothing but his breathing and his stomach gurgling.

"What seems to be the problem?" he asked.

"Why don't you read the clipboard for yourself?" I said sarcastically. "You made me fill it out."

He put his head down, peered through his bifocals, and read.

"Oh dear," he said when he was finished, peering at me over his glasses. "It must be very hard, but I have pills for this."

"Good," I said firmly. "Give them to me in a hurry."

"They won't work right away," he explained. "You must give them three weeks. They'll either make you tired or manic."

Big deal, I thought.

"They will suppress your sex drive," he added, taking off his glasses and rubbing his eyes.

"Now that's a worry," I sneered.

Dr. Horowitz wrote out a prescription for Paxil. He made an appointment for me to see his colleague, Dr. Byron.

∽o∾

The next day in Dr. Byron's office, I could hear his stomach gurgle, just like Horowitz's.

"Tell me about it," he said kindly.

"Read it yourself," I replied, "and tell me what to do."

Dr. Byron read the notes on the clipboard silently and said nothing.

I heard the clock ticking, and waited for him to speak.

When nothing was forthcoming I said, "Well . . ."

"Yes?" he said.

"Should we talk about something?" I asked.

"What would you like to talk about?" he countered.

"Nothing," I said.

The clock continued to tick and the lack of noise in the room made my ears pulse. When the time was up, I made another appointment to come back, but later I canceled it. Dr. Byron's silence and his gurgling stomach made me paranoid.

∽o∾

The pills Dr. Horowitz had prescribed worked, but they gave me hives. When I called and told him, he said to stop taking them immediately. He'd look into finding a new drug for me.

But I didn't want to stop, because even with hives I felt better. I didn't cry as often. I started to think more clearly. I didn't flip out every time Ralph asked me to move his arms, stretch his hands, or pick his nose. I switched to Zoloft. The hives went away. The light-heartedness stayed. Occasionally, I even heard myself sing.

I became an antidepressant missionary. Whenever anybody told me a sad story about pain and heartbreak, I'd say knowingly, "Ahhhh, I have pills for that."

Chapter 14

HISTORY

RALPH'S TWIN BROTHER, RICHARD, came to stay with us. My brother John, who had returned to school in Hayward, and I took off for Yosemite National Park.

We set up our small green tent at Sunnyside Campground. It reminded me of the best times Ralph and I had together, before the accident. The times I tried not to think about now, when we had hiked in the Sierra, skied in the Rockies, climbed in Joshua Tree, kayaked along the coast. The nylon green tent had been our refuge, where we whispered plans and promised to love one another forever, told each other our secrets and our fears, laughed, giggled, made love, ate, read, relaxed, and slept.

I crawled in with my brother and was overwhelmed by the memories that came pouring through the miniature screen window. I started to cry, and my brother decided that it was time he used the outhouse.

❧

When I returned from Yosemite, a new therapist asked me about the past. She wanted to know when and why I had come to California and how I had met Ralph. At first I didn't want to think or talk about it, but gradually I let myself recollect back to 1983, when I had moved west.

After nine years of teaching elementary school in the boonies of western Virginia, I'd packed my little yellow Super Beetle with skis, bicycles, running shoes, backpacks, tents, and climbing gear, and headed toward California to seek my fortune. The sweet but no-good husband I left behind had a law degree and a trust fund, but no job. We'd been married for four years. He didn't want me to go, but he was incapable of stopping me.

My father handed me two hundred dollars as a good-bye present. "Here, sweetheart," he said. "Knock 'em dead in California."

I wound up living in a Pacific Heights broom closet with a wealthy but eccentric woman lawyer. We ran around in her chocolate brown Porsche Targa, looking for love in all the wrong places, until she finally met a nice Jewish doctor and moved to a big house with a view among the comforts of Marin.

After a year of bouncing from job to job—bicycle tour guide, non-Jewish instructor of Russian and Israeli immigrants at the very Orthodox Hebrew Academy of San Francisco, ski bunny in Tahoe, gofer at the *California Law Review* in Sausalito—I decided I needed a vacation.

I headed south of the border, joining forty-five others for a bicycle trip down the Baja Peninsula over the Christmas and New Year holidays. It was the cheapest vacation money could buy, an "active, adventurous travel package," designed for people with too much energy, nowhere to go, and not enough money to do anything first-class. There were thirty-seven men and nine women, four to a room, two to a bed. Of the five single women, I was the last to make reservations, so I was assigned a room with a couple from Oregon and a bald, single guy from New Mexico.

We were supposed to share a bed, but he was scared to death of me. The couple from Oregon made so much noise at night he couldn't sleep.

On Christmas Eve in peaceful Mulege, he flipped out, grabbed the man from Oregon around the throat, and threatened to kill him. Someone bought him a ticket, and he took the slow local bus back to Tijuana.

Several others dropped out along the way because the riding was difficult, the food was evil, and the accommodations were abysmal. As people disappeared, the tour organizer consolidated rooms and reassigned sleeping partners.

No one but I could stand the Oregon couple, so every night a new man rotated into my bed. One night, at Ciudad-Constitution, Ralph rotated in, and he never crawled out.

∽◦∾

At our next session, the therapist asked me to describe what Ralph was like before the accident. Gradually, I began to recall things that had endeared him to me.

I remembered when Ralph took up stained glass making. He had been collecting old Tiffany-style lamps and lamp shades for years and even had a book on antique shades. "Who reads books about lamp shades?" friends asked. No one I knew of except Ralph and his brother, I had to admit.

Ralph found a flyer for a class that advertised "all aspects of stained glass making taught." He went down to the studio and enrolled. At the first night's session, the instructor told the students they'd learn to make tiny window decorations, such as a frog or butterfly or smiley face.

Ralph declared his intention to design a large window for our front door.

"You can't do that," said the teacher.

"Why not?" asked Ralph.

"Because we don't teach window-making in this class," explained the stained glass maker. "This is the beginners' class. We make little decorations you put suction cups on and stick to your kitchen window."

Ralph took the flyer out of his back pocket, unfolded it, and pointed silently to the description, *all aspects of stained glass making taught*. Then he looked at the instructor and said, "I'm making a window for my front door."

He tackled the window the way he approached every project: full tilt, no holds barred. He bought every piece of equipment necessary, read books, and studied the windows of nearby churches and museums. He took over our dining room table and made it his workshop. He redesigned a portion of the garage so that it could contain all the materials he bought. He acquired a license that allowed him to purchase glass at a discount.

His identical twin took up the craft, too. I wasn't surprised. Long ago when Ralph started bike riding and decided that for his first overnight trip he'd ride the length of the Baja Peninsula, Richard went along with him. When Ralph began making beer, he enrolled in a graduate course at U.C. Davis; Richard signed up also. When Ralph and I would arrange to meet Richard in the Eastern Sierra for a backcountry ski trip, he'd show up with the exact same equipment and the same clothes as Ralph. Richard began to accumulate blues music. Ralph did also. Richard collected antique beer trays. So did Ralph. Richard became fanatical about film noir. Ralph became an obsessive fan, too.

Ralph finished his window and installed it in our door. Later, after his body had become useless, the early-morning sun would stream through the small squares, rectangles, and ovals, gold and blue and red. The light filled and warmed our house and made me both happy and sad at the same time.

Ralph forgot about the window. Since it was located at the end of a narrow foyer that led outdoors and to our front steps, he no longer had access to it.

∽○∽

I tried to describe to the therapist what Ralph and I had done before he broke his neck. We skied. We biked. We rock climbed. We rollerbladed and jogged. We hiked, camped, backpacked, and gardened. We went out for nice dinners and cooked fancy meals at home for friends. We bought a house together, filled it with furniture and kitchen gadgets, entertained, and finally got married.

Before the accident, we'd been together twelve years, married for three. We'd gone to the movies twice, seen a play or two, never read the same books, never watched TV. We did activities together. Ralph had the outdoor gear and the skills, and he taught me the things I didn't know. I married him because he was good at all the things I liked to do. And he was just older enough, by thirteen years, that I could keep up with him most of the time.

But all was not perfect. We fought a lot.

The issues we argued over were always the same: how we spent money, how Ralph liked to control things, how I rebelled against his control. I thought Ralph drank too much and was too quick to anger. He thought I stayed too late at work and didn't pay enough attention to details.

I was an admitted slob. He was neat and orderly. He organized piles of stuff into corners. I shoved things into drawers. His T-shirts were folded just so. My clothes looked like an elephant had sat on them. His shirts hung in the closet all precisely facing in the same direction while mine fell to the floor where they were easier to find.

I threatened to leave Ralph a zillion times, and did once for nearly two years. Then I missed his companionship, missed his love of the outdoors, and missed the lovemaking in the bedroom upstairs. I came back.

It looked as though we would stay together. But who can ever tell?

∽o∾

The therapist wanted me to talk more about my past, before I'd moved to California. I wondered how far back she really wanted me to go.

Did she want me to go back to a muggy New Jersey afternoon in 1960 when Donna Richmond told me where babies really came from?

Should I describe my first abortion, the second miscarriage, the third D & C? Did she want to know about my jobs as a chambermaid in 1966, a waitress in 1967, a dog-kennel manager in 1968? How about camp counselor in 1969, lifeguard in 1970, schoolteacher in 1971? Did she want to know that I lived on a Santa Cruz commune in 1971 for less than forty-eight hours; was maced at a Neil Young concert in Boulder in 1972; hitchhiked up the California coast and caught "crabs" from a stranger before heading back east?

I told her I went to Europe and Africa in 1972, graduated without distinction from college in 1974, and moved to California in 1983. I met Ralph in 1984, moved in with him in 1985, traveled in Asia in 1986 and 1987. I got a call from my brother about the accident at 4:03 P.M. on April 27, 1994, and I've been right here, on Dover Street, ever since.

∽∘∾

Shortly after his accident, Ralph's sister sent us a large album she had compiled on the history of the Hager family. In it were photographs of stern-looking German immigrants. Piercing eyes stared out of angular, pale, unsmiling faces at the camera. The men were bearded, the women sturdy. I wasn't surprised by their appearance. I saw it every day when I looked at Ralph.

An entire section was set aside for the birth and life of Ralph and Richard Hager. An article clipped from the *Minneapolis Tribune* explained how experts from the University of Minnesota were studying the identical twin baby sons of Vivian and Walter Hager. The boys had developed their own language in which they communicated with each other. Gene specialists from around the country found them fascinating.

A later article pictured two fair-haired identical twins with butterfly nets. The news clipping said that the eleven-year-old Hager brothers had been capturing butterflies for more than four years. Their collection, the most comprehensive catalogue of butterflies in the entire state, was now exhibited at the Museum of Natural History in Minneapolis. No one had seen an inventory quite like it.

On the next page, a headline shouted TWINS GRADUATE VALEDICTORIANS. A photograph of Ralph and Richard, now teenagers, depicted them studying at matching desks in a comfortable room surrounded by globes, model airplanes, college pennants, and preserved butterflies. The article said that the Hager brothers, identical twins and best friends, had received straight A's throughout junior high and high school. They also had won an award for perfect attendance, having never missed a day of school in their lives. The following September, they would enroll at the University of Minnesota, where each would study mathematics, engineering, and physics.

∽o∾

Richard and I had always had a love-hate relationship.

I had come from a family where everyone resolved problems by yelling and screaming at one another. Richard and Ralph never showed such emotions. They were oblivious to everything but their own circle of belongings, hobbies, and obsessions. In Richard, Ralph had the perfect soulmate, a brother who talked and walked and acted just as he did. They could finish each other's sentences and thoughts. They understood each other completely, simply, essentially.

As a professor of mathematics at San Diego State University for the past twenty-five years, Richard was set in his ways. He'd been divorced for over twenty years, since his wife and their three small daughters had left. He lived in a house overflowing with collections of African masks, beer paraphernalia, antique records, and old sheet music.

Before the accident, Ralph had been the dominant one. After the accident, Richard took over, setting up the electronic communications systems upon which Ralph depended.

More than once, an old friend would come in the back door, see Richard standing in the kitchen, think it was Ralph recovered from his quadriplegia, and go into shock. They were that much alike. It was creepy.

Richard did not discuss, he lectured. He couldn't answer a question Yes or No or Maybe without giving the background on a hundred other subjects.

The house was never clean enough for him. I put things

away in places that didn't make logical sense, he said. I was letting the vines outside go wild; the knives in the kitchen were all dull; the drawers everywhere were disorganized; Ralph's toolbox was a mess.

Trashcans overflowed in every corner; newspapers were piled up on the floor; there were no lids for the Tupperware containers.

But worst of all, there was never enough good beer in the refrigerator. Everything in and around the house was screwed up because of me.

When Richard came to visit, I stayed away as much as possible.

∽o∾

Another therapist asked me to write down all the reasons I had married Ralph. Maybe it would help me understand why I was with him now.

I got out a piece a paper and wrote down the following:

Able to fix the car.
Owned gear for climbing, mountaineering, backcountry skiing.
Able to repair derailleurs, brakes, and flat tires on bicycles.
Kept garage well supplied with spare tubes and parts and camping gear.
Did all the grocery shopping.
Did all the planning of meals and cooking.
Kept lists of things we needed to buy.
Kept records of when the car needed its oil changed and then changed it.
Ran all errands on Saturdays.

Kept the house supplied with paper and pencils and envelopes; never lost pen caps.

Knew how to choose and use a computer and software and all that stuff.

Did our taxes and paid our bills.

Purchased good cooking pots, sharp knives, and interesting kitchen gadgets.

Could rewire things that were broken.

Was neat and organized; had a place for everything.

Kept his clothes folded and ironed and clean.

Sewed his own buttons and patched his own pants.

Liked to go out for dinner at nice restaurants.

Liked to do the same things I did.

Wasn't too mushy, too sentimental, too touchy-feely.

Was relatively attentive in bed.

Made my knees weak when I hadn't seen him in a while.

Liked my career choice, my friends, my tenacity.

Allowed me to do most of the things I wanted to do.

Dressed neatly and stylishly and with a bit of flair.

Was thin, in shape, and in excellent health.

Liked to go to parties and socialize and dance and do things with other people.

Had a good secure job, made decent money, had full health coverage.

Was an enthusiast for interior decorating.

Was a collector and interested in a variety of things: pre-Columbian art; antique sign memorabilia; Oriental rugs; old beer stuff; stained glass lamps and shades; jazz and classical music; wines from the sixties.

Made good beer and beautiful windows.

Took the Boy Scouts on canoe and ski trips.

Could ride his bike farther and telemark ski better than most men half his age.

Wasn't a womanizer or a flirt or a bullshitter.

Never worried or procrastinated or gossiped about other people.

Had an excellent education; could figure out mathematical equations no one else could.

Was smart and eccentric and loved me to pieces.

I looked at the list. Only the last item made any sense now.

When the therapist asked me to write down the personality traits I hadn't liked about Ralph before his accident, I jotted down the following: bad temper, selfish, self-centered, unable to save money, poor sense of humor, boring conversationalist, crummy dancer.

Then she wanted me to list the worst things that ever happened to me. I wrote:

Ralph's accident.

Leaving a job I loved before I got demoted.

Getting fired from my ski-bunny job.

Having three miscarriages.

Not being able to get pregnant and stay pregnant.

Having the neighborhood babysitter force me to stroke his penis.

Seeing a guy's pecker through a car window when I didn't want to see it.

Having to turn down a date with the captain of the football team because I had a date with someone else.

That was it. Maybe it hadn't been such a bad life after all.

Chapter 15

First Christmas

It was two days before Christmas, around 10 P.M., when I decided we needed to get the tree. It was our first Christmas since the accident. We were almost eight months into our new life. My antidepressants had kicked in, and I was starting to get the holiday spirit. It was time to get the tree.

There was no place to go but Pac n' Save. Mrs. Scott, who had now been presiding over our home for the past few months, was frying chicken in the kitchen.

"Let's go, Scott," I said, "we gotta get the tree."

"Okay, baby, let me jus' finish puttin' this food up and I'll be ready. What else we need to get?"

Everything: a stiff drink, a shot of heroin, a million dollars, a bullet through the head. What did we need?

We jumped in the van. Well, we didn't really jump. Mrs. Scott rolled her big soft body in and panted heavily. She had the seat permanently back as far as it would go, but she still didn't have enough room. The seat belt didn't fit around her belly.

"Baby, you know what you need?" she asked as I backed out of our driveway.

"What?" I mumbled distractedly, turning the van toward 51st Street.

"Some dick, baby, some dick."

"MRS. SCOTT!" I stopped short at an intersection.

"I know, I know. Now don't go gettin' upset. It just that it ain't right, baby, you bein' young and all, with that disabled husband of yours in the house. A young woman like you needs some dick."

"Mrs. Scott," I said, "come on. We have to drive the van to Pac n' Save and buy a Christmas tree. Let's not discuss this now."

"I know it, I know it." Her voice was soft and conspiratorial. "I just know you gotta have some good lovin' or your pussy will all dry up and that ain't no good for a young woman like you. I ain't need no dick, but I'm an old woman and I don't need no man puttin' somethin' where it don't belong no more. Gettin' all down and funky. But you need some dick. What else we gonna buy at the store?"

"Nothing," I said. "We haven't got any money for anything but the tree."

"Oh Lordy, baby, you know we need some stuff. I need cake flour and eggs and sour cream and butter."

It was a mob scene at the store. A year before, I wouldn't have gone near this place so close to Christmas. I would have been out of town, skiing down a white snowy slope, lying on a sandy beach, riding a bicycle along a dusty Mexican path.

But this year I was happy to be five minutes out of the house, listening to tinny Christmas carols blaring from the store's loudspeaker, fighting for a parking space, squeezing my eyes half shut so the Christmas lights looked like stars. I glanced over at my new best friend, Mrs. Scott. Three hundred pounds of soft flesh sat uncomfortably in the velour seat of the van with the lift in the back. They called these seats captain's chairs. Mrs. Scott had become my captain.

I pulled the van into the last disabled space left in the lot.

"Let's go, baby," commanded my captain.

We got out of the van. Mrs. Scott limped across the parking lot, greeting everyone who walked by.

"Hello, sistah. My, you look beautiful today."

"What you got there, baby? My, my, Suze, we gotta get us some of that!"

At the store entrance, Mrs. Scott waited while I found a quarter to pay for a cart. Then she took over, as she always did. She entered Pac n' Save as if she were Queen for a Day. She started filling the cart with stuff. Some of it we needed, some of it we didn't.

First the greens; then the bacon and chicken; then toilet tissue, coffee filters, and paper towels.

A few months earlier, I had realized Mrs. Scott liked to move real slow around the store, selecting the most expensive brands. It made her feel wealthy. My job was to follow her and put back the items we didn't need, like giant jars of pickles, cans of white and red kidney beans, applesauce, crushed pineapple, bags of white rice, and multiple boxes of butter. We needed one package of ham hocks, not two; two packages of hot links, not three. Maybe because of the new diet she had me on—fat, cholesterol, pig parts, and pound cake—I didn't seem to have the energy to tell her no. The cart got full, and then more full.

I had to stop her. "Scotty, let's get out of here and go get the tree," I pleaded. The Christmas spirit at Pac n' Save was starting to get on my nerves.

We headed over to the temporary tree section. There weren't many left, but the selection smelled good. I realized I wasn't really looking for a tree, just the tip of one that would fit on a table. There wasn't much room in a house full of bedpans, syringes, adult diapers, and ham hocks.

The sinewy young men working the graveyard shift of the

Christmas tree department were looking mean and surly. They wore black wool caps advertising malt liquor pushed down around their eyebrows.

We found a selection of little treetops. Mrs. Scott was about three times larger than any one tree and twice as wide as any of the young men hustling about.

"What you want, Momma?" one said to her. He couldn't see me standing behind her.

I walked around, looked over the merchandise, and picked out a skinny half-dead treetop. Then we headed back to the van. I had the tree in my arms. Mrs. Scott was behind me, in charge of the cart, as always. I was starting to feel light-hearted. Shoppers rushed by. The loudspeaker blared "Jingle Bell Rock."

"Hey, Scotty," I called to Mrs. Scott. "Aren't you getting a tree?"

"Honey, I am the Christmas tree," she shouted, her voice booming across the expanse between us.

I looked at her: big hoop earrings; gold lamé cap; green, orange, and purple coat over a black-and-red striped blouse; flowered skirt spread across a pair of lime green–checked stretch pants; gold slippers on her feet; and a loopy string of plastic pearls around her neck.

She was right. She was the Christmas tree. She smelled of Pine-Sol and lily of the valley eau de toilette. Her trunk was massive and sturdy. Her limbs were heavy, bending, and protective. She was adorned with tinsel and beads and bric-a-brac. There was no need for an angel to crown her cap. She was that angel. She was everything good and pure and innocent that Christmas represents, and at that moment I loved her more than I loved anybody else on earth.

Chapter 16

AFTER CHRISTMAS

I FELT THAT I might finally be able to look for employment. Money was tight. Jerry was working seven days a week for us, getting Ralph up in the morning and putting him to bed at night. I knew that we would eventually have to find someone else to assist with the work load, but for now Jerry was satisfied. Plus, we couldn't really afford another attendant.

Mrs. Scott was helping me during the day—and, to tell the truth, I needed to get out of the house, not just to pull away from the daily responsibilities of taking care of Ralph but to get out from under Mrs. Scott's constant mothering.

Before Ralph's accident, we had belonged to an indoor climbing gym in San Francisco. I needed work that was distracting, nearby, and flexible. The climbing gym was looking for someone to do part-time promotional work. It seemed a perfect arrangement.

As long as I could get up in the morning and fool myself into a normal routine of making breakfast, reading the paper, and leaving for work, I felt that I could handle the surreal quality of my new life. I could come home and face the task of preparing dinner and feeding Ralph. If I could exhaust myself at work, then I could bear the tedium of evenings at home watching TV. Mrs. Scott was not happy that I would be gone during the day, but even she knew that if I didn't get outside once in a while, I'd go stark raving mad.

But something else was bothering me. Just over eight months had passed since the accident. I hadn't attempted to have intimacy with Ralph since that first week home from the hospital. I was crazy for some form of physical contact. There were days when I just needed a hug. Sometimes, I wanted to climb up into Mrs. Scott's huge, soft lap and let her rock me like a baby. I was becoming possessed with thoughts of sex. Mrs. Scott was right. I needed to get laid. Badly.

∾◦∾

One morning, heading out the back door in my jogging shorts and T-shirt, I almost ran into Jerry in the kitchen.

"Whoa, baby, don't you look good!" he exclaimed, looking me up and down.

I couldn't remember when anyone had last said anything to me besides "You're doing a great job, I don't know how you do it."

I looked up into his face, and for the first time I noticed that his eyes were bright and green and they were looking at me in a way that made the lower half of my body feel like pudding.

I was speechless. Jerry went about the business of taking care of Ralph.

I went for my run and thought about him for the next six miles, as I ran by the post office, the library and the Pac n' Save.

∾◦∾

I became obsessed with Jerry and thoughts of sex. I watched him as he worked with Ralph. Suddenly, he didn't look so old and tired and overweight. Now he appeared robust, healthy, and strong. His arms were huge and everything looked solid and muscular. I joked around with him in the kitchen and tortured myself at nights with thoughts of him in the other room waiting for me.

One day, Ralph asked us to move some items into the attic for him. I could feel my heart pounding as Jerry followed me upstairs, both of us carrying a box of old books and magazines. We looked up at the small opening above the middle bedroom door frame.

"Come on," Jerry said, lacing his fingers together to make a step. "I'll boost you up there. Then I'll hand you the boxes." I stepped into Jerry's palms, and with a powerful motion, he propelled me up into the attic. He has to be looking up my shorts, I thought as I crawled into the dark space. I reached down to take each box from his outstretched hands, avoiding his eyes. When I came down, he guided me onto his shoulders. My legs were wrapped around his warm, thick neck and his bare arms held my naked thighs. I was breathless.

But he never made any overture that I could interpret as blatantly wanting me. I was sure he did, but I was afraid if I let him know how I was feeling, I might scare him away. I wasn't prepared to be rejected by a sixty-year-old black man with tattoos and a gold earring. Miss Manners hadn't answered any letters lately on the appropriate way to sleep with one's live-in employee.

Finally I couldn't stand it any longer. One night, I stood outside Jerry's bedroom in my sexiest T-shirt waiting for a sign from God that I should go in. It didn't come. I went back to bed, got up, and went to the door again. All I could hear was snoring. I returned to bed, then rose and tiptoed to the closed door. This time, I put my hand on the doorknob before I gave up. My head and heart were pounding.

Back to bed again, then up again. Finally, I grabbed the doorknob, opened the door, and rushed in. The snoring stopped. I crawled into the left side of the bed and lay down. Jerry rolled over and put his arm around me.

"Jerry, I need a favor," I whispered. That's all I said. Jerry didn't say anything. His hands were all the reply I needed.

∽o∾

During those first few months of sleeping with Jerry, I began to wonder about my sanity. As I got to know him more intimately, I questioned the values on which I had been raised and the vows I had said on my wedding day. What in hell was I doing? I couldn't explain it to myself or to anyone else. The few friends I took into my confidence were appalled. Many feared for my safety, for my health, and for Ralph's well-being. But Ralph was so overwhelmed by mysterious pain and a complicated drug regimen, he had little time to pay attention to me or Jerry.

I became more accustomed to the sleeping arrangement upstairs. I no longer spent time in the back bedroom or on the living room couch in my street clothes. Every night I lay naked in bed beside Jerry.

His warm, smooth body felt incredibly comforting. When he put his massive, muscular arms around me, I felt small, vulnerable and safe. He told me street jokes and made me laugh. He definitely knew what he was doing when it came to lovemaking. I started to feel better, more attractive, sexier. I began to relax.

Still, sleeping with Jerry was troubling. I felt sorry for Ralph, dishonest, confused. But Jerry's attentions helped me get through the day-to-day struggle. I didn't want to hurt my husband, but there were certain things I needed that he could no longer give me. Intimacy with Jerry seemed a convenient, almost effortless, solution. I didn't have to go outside our home looking for physical companionship. Instead, I was home every night after work, sometimes even early.

Chapter 17

The Benefit

At some point during the first winter after the accident, friends came up with the idea of a benefit for Ralph and me. Although we were embarrassed by their concern and generosity, we accepted their proposal with enthusiasm. We weren't sure how we were going to pay our bills.

The date was set for February 4.

Mrs. Scott insisted on being involved. She wanted to host a quilt show at our house. She said we should put a shoe box at a table by the front door, charge people admission, and send them through the hallway, and into the dining room. There they could meet Ralph, look at the quilts, walk through the French doors back into the hallway again, and leave through the front door. She had made a whole pile of money on quilt shows. We could do the same.

It took several dinners of fried chicken and ham hocks to convince her that we didn't want to raise money her way. We would have a benefit at the gym where I was working occasionally. People would come to hear music, watch a dance performance, bid in a silent auction. Mrs. Scott could raffle off her quilts.

She accepted the challenge and commenced to sewing and directing her friends: Mrs. Bueller and Mrs. Cooper, Miz Lucky and Miz Glady, Dee Dee and the rest of the neighborhood women.

As the day of the benefit approached, Mrs. Scott grew more and more frenzied. She made pillowcases, mini-afghans, and weird little fabric squares whose purpose was unclear. She cooked pies and cakes and cookies and stocked up on supplies for the big day. She had me run in the morning to the fabric store, in the afternoon to the Pac n' Save, and in the evening to the pharmacy for her heart pills and gout medicine. Some days, she didn't get out of her nightgown and slippers or put in her teeth until noon.

My father flew in from Philadelphia, my brother Bill came from Atlantic City. My friends Laurie and Jenny arrived from New York City. Sally came from Washington, D.C. Ralph's brother drove up from San Diego.

∽∘∾

Mrs. Scott could not be stopped. She made ten pounds of potato salad, three plates of fried chicken, ribs soaked in sauce, cornbread, and bread pudding. She had posted her own invitations, and she sent my brother Bill out to collect her friends.

They all arrived at the benefit early in gold lamé and black stockings, ruffles and velvet, pins and bows. Mrs. Cooper had on her wig, slightly cockeyed. Miz Lucky was engulfed in an enormous purple hat festooned with pink ostrich feathers. Miz Glady was covered in lace, from beret to pumps. Mrs. Jefferson, the practical one, wore a flowered dress and sturdy brown shoes. She could actually walk without help, unlike the others who needed extra assistance in their high heels. Mrs. Scott was decked out in a long black-velvet evening ensemble with a matching satin top and a size 44 gold-threaded velveteen jacket.

Throughout the evening, there was plenty of drinking and dancing and speech making. Friends and acquaintances purchased many raffle tickets and placed bids for the quilt Mrs. Scott had sewn together from dozens of neckties and Mrs. Cooper and Mrs. Jefferson had quilted.

Late in the evening, the lights went dim and the room became silent. Mrs. Scott sang "If I Could Help Someone" in that enormous, wild voice of hers. There wasn't a dry eye in the house. She grabbed hold of the microphone and gave the audience her views on the importance of friendship, followed by a lecture on quilting and the high price of fabric and thread and groceries. Finally, someone gently took the microphone away from her and turned up the rap music. Mrs. Scott took her big old body out on the dance floor and began to rock.

∾∘∾

The benefit raised almost thirty thousand dollars. We were overwhelmed by the generosity of friends and strangers. Al, a former co-worker of Ralph's, put the money in a joint account under both our names.

The fund was for attendant care, but $30,000 would run out in less than a year. We set it aside as backup. I continued to pay Jerry out of my savings. When I went back to work full-time, I was happy to give my entire paycheck over to Ralph's help. After all, it was my ticket to the outside world.

Ralph paid the rest of the household bills with his pension. The voice-activated computer system Richard had set up for Ralph allowed him to write checks, electronically withdraw money, and complete our tax forms. It was good to see him active, taking authority over some aspects of our lives.

Several months after the benefit, I came home from work and learned that Ralph had withdrawn all the benefit money and invested it in the stock market. For days, we watched the market go up and down, down and up, and then finally down.

It was not a good time for us. I was very angry.

"At least we could have paid back my parents for the van they bought us," I declared.

Ralph didn't answer me.

"At least you could pay me back the ten thousand dollars I spent out of my savings while you were in the hospital."

Ralph remained quiet.

"You could have at least consulted a stockbroker or someone who knew something about the market before doing this."

Silence.

"We could have remodeled the bathroom for you, or bought an electric door, so we all don't have to hang around here every day and wait and see if you want to go out or come in."

More silence.

But the money had been spent. The market didn't exactly crash. We'd just have to wait for it to go up again. We weren't going anywhere, anyway. I tried to be an optimist. "It will come back," I told myself.

Chapter 18

MORE THERAPY

I TOLD MY LATEST therapist that I worked in an indoor climbing gym. "Everyone in the gym is young, muscular, thin, and obsessed with physical fitness, the exact opposite of Ralph, Jerry, and Mrs. Scott," I said.

My therapist seemed fixated on finding out why I worked in such a place.

"My boss gives me absolute flexibility," I explained.

"I see," he said thoughtfully.

"It's an escape," I continued. "The entire San Francisco Bay separates me from my problems. A big body of water that can't be crossed except by a bridge and only during times of light traffic. A reverse commute. It's not so bad."

"Mmmm," he mumbled, pressing his fingers together, studying his perfectly manicured nails.

"It's not good money, but it's relaxed. I don't have to wear panty hose. I make my own hours. I get to do lots of different things. I clean the bathrooms, take out the trash. I am in charge of lost and found."

"Yes," he said gravely, "but what about all those young men?"

"What young men?"

"The climbers at the gym. Are you attracted to them? Do

they know you are attracted to them? Do they know you want them?"

"Do I want them? No, I don't want them. I'm into big, bad, older black men. Haven't you been listening to me?"

∽∽∽

When I missed a session with the therapist—I went the day after the appointed date—I knew I'd made an unconscious effort to ditch him.

I rushed into the office, breathless, for what I thought was a 2 P.M. Wednesday meeting.

"I'm sorry, it was yesterday," said the receptionist.

I stared at her wild-eyed. I felt unbalanced. She could see that I was desperate.

"You know," she said, "Dr. Watson has an appointment right now that is about to end. Why don't you go upstairs, wait for him, and see if he will see you now? Or you can make an appointment with him for sometime soon."

She smiled. I knew she felt sorry for me.

I went upstairs and waited by Dr. Watson's closed door for nearly fifteen minutes. As he came out, he glanced at me. Then he proceeded to walk down the hall.

"Excuse me, Dr. Watson," I said as I followed him, "we had an appointment yesterday. I missed it. I want to reschedule. The receptionist said you might be able to see me now, or soon."

Dr. Watson turned and looked at me. His eyes tried to focus. I could tell he had no idea who I was, even though I had told him every dark, dirty secret of my life. He didn't have a clue.

"Oh," he said. "Go down to the front desk. Make an appointment with the receptionist. She knows my schedule."

And with that he turned on his heels and continued walking down the hallway without me.

I didn't make the appointment. I didn't go back to his office again. I didn't give him another thought or a second glance. I wasn't going to tell him anything more about me, that was for sure. It was too hot in that building anyway.

∽⌒∾

Ralph and I went to a couples therapist. She asked Ralph to apologize to me.

"What for?" I asked.

"For having a bicycle accident and changing your life forever," she explained.

Before Ralph could answer, I said, "Look, it was an accident. Ralph doesn't need to apologize to me. Accidents happen."

I turned to Ralph. "Ralph, you don't need to apologize to me. It wasn't your fault."

Ralph looked at me with his once-bright blue eyes, now cloudy from drugs. His salt-and-pepper hair needed to be cut and styled. His beard was overgrown and wild. The plaid cap he once wore so jauntily upon his head sagged sadly. "Suzy," he whispered, his voice hoarse. "I will if it's important to you."

"Don't bother, Ralph," I answered firmly. "It's not necessary."

The couples therapist kept digging. She wanted to know the level of intimacy between Ralph and me.

I tried to steer her away from the subject. "What's the point?" I asked sarcastically. "Ralph doesn't think about it. He's got far bigger challenges than sex. It's not important. It's not even possible."

"Oh, but it is," she chirped. "You just need to figure out a schedule and a new way of doing things. There are definitely ways to do this. We need to explore the options."

Lady, I thought, get a grip. What you read in psychology textbooks is not necessarily true. I touch Ralph and he goes into spasms. His breath smells ferocious. He's surrounded by so much metal and plastic on his wheelchair that it's impossible to get close to him. He has far more important things than sex to think about. And me, well, I'm just too tired. Leave it alone, will you please?

But the therapist was determined to help. She began a lecture. I looked over at Ralph. His eyes were glazed. He was in that space where he was neither conscious nor unconscious, neither asleep nor awake. I wished that I was there with him. I wanted the therapist to shut up.

"What is your day like?" she asked. "Tell me about it so we can work out a plan for you and Ralph. We need to get you back together in the physical sense." She chuckled nervously.

I hesitated for a moment. "All right. I'll tell you about yesterday, how's that? It was a typical day. Here's what happened after I came home from picking up a prescription for Ralph at the pharmacy:

"Jerry had the afternoon off so I washed the breakfast dishes, folded the laundry, paid an overdue credit card bill, and spread the paper out on the dining room table for Ralph to read. I leaned over him to give him a kiss on the cheek and as I did so, I smelled something foul. I put my hands between his legs and felt his trousers. His pants were soaked. I needed to change his clothes. I disengaged the gears of the wheelchair and pushed it into our living room, which is now Ralph's bedroom. I removed his glasses, his mouth stick, and the tray on which he rests his hands. I turned off the control buttons and bent the electric box and the joystick away from Ralph's face. I got down on my hands and knees, cranked up the hospital bed, and reached under the wheelchair to unlatch the footrests. I laid a rubber sheet on the bed, slammed the safety rails down, and yanked the wheelchair armrests out of their sockets. I straddled Ralph's knees, unhooked his chest strap and belt, and unbuttoned his shirt. I raised his arms and lifted the shirt over his head. I pulled it off his body, one sleeve at a time. I reached for the wooden slide board, leaned Ralph as far to the right as I dared, and shoved the board under his wet buttocks. I sat him back down on the board, clenched my knees hard around his thighs, and rocked him side to side. Taking a deep breath, I slid him with all my might onto the bed. Practically on top of Ralph, I pushed and shoved his body across the rubber sheet until I was sure he was safe. I wound up sprawled on top of my helpless, wet husband."

I looked at the therapist. She was staring down at her notebook, chewing on the end of her pen. I glanced over at Ralph. He was sleeping.

"Listen," I whispered. "I'm taking care of this intimacy thing in my own way and I don't want to lie to Ralph."

And with that small remark, she quit being our therapist. She told Ralph and me at our next meeting that I had disclosed something that made it impossible for her to work with us as a couple. We went home discouraged. We had liked her and felt, for once, we were getting some help. But Ralph never asked me what I had confided to her. He was too busy with other, more pressing problems.

∽o∾

A friend suggested that I see a massage therapist. Normally, I wouldn't bother with such treatment. But I was so full of anger, so incredibly depressed, I thought I needed to augment the Zoloft in some way.

Ginger gave me June's telephone number and I made an appointment.

A few days later, I went to a stucco bungalow in Berkeley.

A tiny rock garden out front was overflowing with native plants. Inside, the house was full of dappled golden light. June, a short, wide woman dressed in a flowing caftan, took me to a small, quiet room. She asked me to remove my clothes and lie on the massage table. Then she left me alone.

Gentle music played, sounding like the ocean. Incense burned on a table that held seashells, dried flowers, and a few bleached bones. I covered myself with a thin, cool sheet and waited for her return.

June came into the room softly. She asked me to take a few deep breaths and to exhale slowly. As I did so, she took several enormous, loud, measured breaths herself, and exhaled onto my body. At first I felt frightened, but she told me to relax and breathe more deeply. I closed my eyes and concentrated on letting go of my anger.

June wrapped her strong, oiled hands around my calves and worked her fingers into the flesh, deeper and deeper, then she moved down to my feet and toes, then up the length of my legs to my thighs. All the while, she breathed intensely and exhaled onto my body. It felt surprisingly good, like a warm breeze against my skin. I faded in and out of consciousness, as June whispered to me, asking me to relax and then to turn over.

I don't remember how long June worked on my body, but when she was through, she asked me to get dressed and meet her on her back porch.

As I rose off the table, I felt rejuvenated. I moved slowly and deliberately, each action flowing into the next.

I found June waiting for me on her deck above a flower-filled backyard. She handed me a glass of water and instructed me to drink.

"Suzy," she began, "you are so full of hostility you are on the verge of exploding. Your liver is about to go. It may be tomor-

row, next year, five years from now. I don't know when. But I
do know that you are storing all your frustrations and anger
there. It won't be able to hold it much longer.

"I think I pulled a lot of rage out of you. That's why I was
doing so much breath work. But there is still much more there
and you are going to need help to get it all out. You need to join
a yoga group. You need to take blue-green algae tablets daily.
Today and every day, I recommend that you drink lots of water,
stay out of the sun, and try to slow down. You may find yourself
crying uncontrollably at times. Let it happen. That's your body
letting out some of its madness."

I settled up my bill with June and went out into the bright
sunlight. I got into my car and drove home. As I fought for position on busy Martin Luther King Jr. Way, I thought about what
June had said. She was right about a lot of things. But there was
one thing I was certain she had gotten wrong. I wasn't storing
the anger in my liver. I was holding it in my heart.

A new shrink told me I was sleeping with Jerry because I was a
risk-taker. She was my age, white, and, I concluded, unmarried
and timid. Others, more graciously, might have called her cautious.

I'd taken risks all my life, she thought—and Jerry was
another one, akin to skiing down a black diamond run, climbing Mount Rainier, living in my neighborhood in North Oakland. When she told me that she had never been to the
mountains or seen snow, I knew that we were not a good
match.

"I think you are a risk-taker," she repeated.

"Look," I said, "we've been over this before. I'm scared
to death. I can hardly get up in the morning, I'm so afraid of

what's going to happen. Sleeping with Jerry isn't a risk. It's a necessity. I need somebody to hold me, to tell me I'm beautiful and smart and sexy. Everybody needs it. I'm just getting it in the most easy, economical, and only way I can. It's not risky, it's human nature."

"Mmmmmm," she said.

"Would it be better if I went somewhere else to get it? Mrs. Scott? I don't think so. I've thought about a relationship with a woman, but to me that's more risky. I'd have to leave the house. I could get very confused. I might not ever come back."

"But what about your plans to have a baby?"

What about it, I thought. What possible alternatives are there?

"Well," I stammered, "having a baby now is completely out of the question. And adoption, well I've thought about it, but what kind of life would it be for a child to be in such a chaotic, dysfunctional family, with one guardian disabled and another fucking insane?"

"Yes," she said.

"You know," I said hesitantly, "I've thought about having a baby with Jerry. I really have. It's clear that he can make them. I know it's crazy, but . . ."

The therapist began to fidget. She pressed her fingers together in front of her mouth and made little push-up movements with her hands. We stared at each other.

"You are a risk-taker," she said again, quietly.

"Tell me what to do," I pleaded. "Please. Tell me. I'm lost."

"I can't tell you what to do. I can only help you explore the new options that are now before you."

"I don't want options," I blubbered. "I want answers. I want someone to tell me what Ralph and I should do! I can't figure it out on my own."

I started to cry and she handed me a box of tissues. "This is stupid," I mumbled into a Kleenex. "I need help, but nobody has the answers."

"It's hard," she said.

Jesus, I thought, you've got that right. But what possible use is all this talking? Better not to think about it. Better to take my pills, get up in the morning, go to work, and exhaust myself. Besides, why am I telling you all this? You've never even seen snow.

The therapist let me cry for a while. Then the clock ran out. I made another appointment, but when it came time to go back, I didn't keep it. I knew that no one was going to be able to tell me what to do. I would have to figure it out on my own.

Chapter 19

THE OPTIONS THAT ARE NOW BEFORE YOU

My FRIEND KRISTEN, WHO had introduced us to Jerry, was looking for a man for herself in the personals section of the East Bay Express, but she wasn't having any luck. When I told her what Jerry and I were up to, she said, "No, I'm sorry, but that just won't do. We can do better than that."

So each week, after looking through the Men Seeking Women columns, she turned to Special Situations and looked for someone for me.

"I found him," she shouted into the telephone one morning.

"Who?" I asked.

"A guy for you."

"Kristen," I reminded her, "I've got a guy. And a husband. I'm all squared away. You don't have to help me."

"Oh, but I want to. Listen to this. It's under Special Situations. *MWNSP in a sexless marriage due to disability seeks understanding female for special relationship.* I've already listened to his recorded message. He sounds nice. His wife has rheumatism. They haven't had meaningful sex in seven years."

I paused for just a moment. "Give me the number," I said. "I'll call him."

I dialed the mailbox number and listened while a deeply

depressed voice said, "Hello, I'm in a sexless marriage. My wife has congenital rheumatism. I'm looking for companionship and more."

I hung up the telephone before the message was finished and called Kristen. "Okay," I said. "What do I do now?"

"Call him back and leave a message. Come over and we'll do it together."

Jerry was getting Ralph readied for the day so I ran up to Kristen's house, and together we went over the instructions on how to leave a reply for a personal ad. We composed a script of what I would say. I called the man from the personals and left my message on his mailbox number.

I waited and waited, but I never heard from him.

But I didn't care. I already had a husband and a boyfriend.

‿o‿

My Slavic friend Lenore, who had a marriage of convenience with a transvestite named Frank, alias Francile, was adamant that I explore a relationship with a woman. She was not enamored with the idea that I slept with Jerry. She was, in fact, appalled, a reaction I found surprising considering her own state of affairs.

"My marriage to Frank is for green-card status only," she explained defensively. "I'm completely faithful to Marion. It's nothing like your relationship with Ralph and Jerry."

It was Lenore who insisted I get an AIDS test and Lenore who gave me a large paper sack full of exra-large condoms, just in case. She sent me a catalog of sexual gizmos that she hinted were better than the real thing, and she recommended that I meet her at Good Vibrations, an adult toy shop in San Francisco, to consider other options.

I wormed my way out of our research date and said no to her invitations for me to join her, Frank, and Marion some weekend along the Russian River. Eventually I ran out of excuses. I agreed to meet her at a club in San Francisco.

I told Ralph and Jerry I was having dinner with Lenore and her friends. I drove over the Bay Bridge and slunk with trepidation into a dark dance hall at Howard and 8th streets. The place was jammed with women in polyester pants. Lenore was not hard to find. Surrounded by admirers, she stood at the center of the dance floor, twirling around under a pulsing strobe light, dressed in striped Cat in the Hat pants and a tiny lime green tube top.

I pushed through the crowd, looking for the bar. But the disco music was too loud and the atmosphere not all that inviting, so instead I headed straight out of the place. I went home and crawled into bed with Jerry.

"How was it?" he mumbled into his pillow.

"Oh, okay I guess, but I'm tired." I sighed.

"How were the lesbians?" he asked.

"What lesbians?"

"The ones you been with tonight."

"How'd you know about them?"

"Baby," Jerry said, turning on his side and looking at me. "I know everything you do. You ain't got no secrets from me. Now come on over here and let me show you what a real man can do. You don't need no help from anyone else. I'm the only thing you need."

"Oh yeah?"

"Oh yeah, girl, you better believe it," he said, putting his huge arm around my waist and pulling me toward him. "I'm the only thing you need."

Chapter 20

STANDING IN LINE

I WAS GOING TO the pharmacy practically every day. And each time I went, I encountered a new set of instructions and a new bundle of frustration.

The pharmacies at Kaiser were in transition, encouraging members to order prescriptions by telephone and have them delivered to their homes. I tried ordering drugs by telephone for Ralph, and they weren't always delivered. I had to haul myself down to the hospital and beg for holdover pills until the pharmacy got its act together and filled my order.

One week, I went to Kaiser Monday, Tuesday, and Wednesday. On Monday, I picked up holdover pills for a prescription that had not been delivered. On Tuesday, I went back to pick up the prescription. It wasn't ready. I returned on Wednesday in a bad mood.

There was new signage on the walls. In fact, there were four new signs: a sign for ordering pills, a sign for picking up pills ordered by a doctor, a sign for telephone orders, and one that mysteriously said 24-HR MEMBER PHONE-IN REFILL EXPRESS LINE. PICK-UP ONLY. But there was a problem. There were four signs but only three lines marked on the floor to stand behind. I knew about these lines. I'd been told by the clerks in the past to stand behind them and not come to the counter until called. And so, on Wednesday, when I entered the pharmacy and saw the four new signs, I looked to find the line I was supposed to stand behind. I had to make a decision. Should I stand behind a line, or in front of a sign? They didn't all match up. I looked around. Everyone was standing behind a line. Four signs, three lines. I stood behind a painted line where no one else was waiting.

"You aren't in line," a clerk yelled in my direction after what seemed like an interminable wait. I looked behind and around me to see whom she was yelling at. "You," she said, looking right at me. "You aren't in a line."

I looked down at the line in front of me, at the woman who had followed my lead and stood behind me, up at the sign that was not quite in front of me but slightly to my left.

"I'm behind a line," I protested quietly.

"Come up here," she answered.

I walked across the painted line I had so obediently stood behind. "Nobody helped you 'cause you weren't in a line," she repeated loud enough for everyone in the room to hear.

"But what about the line on the floor?" I asked.

"That doesn't mean anything," she said. "It's been changed. You need to stand in front of one of these signs." She pointed above her head with a perfectly manicured finger.

"You need a sign that says to ignore the lines and only look at the signs," I answered, suddenly angry. "Or you need to paint one more line to match up with the signs. Or you need to remove the three lines you already have that apparently don't mean anything."

"I'm not here to argue with you," she said.

"Fine," I answered, my voice escalating. "Go get your manager."

Just then someone in front of a sign, but not behind a line, shouted, "Get a life, lady."

"I have one already, thank you," I answered, but deep down in my gut I wasn't quite sure. My face was hot and burning and my head felt as if it would explode.

Some people need Jesus, I thought. Some follow Mohammed, and others crave alcohol, sex, and rock and roll. Maybe I'm the kind of person who requires a line to stand behind and a sign to tell me what to do.

Chapter 21

FALLING APART

Rachel, WHO STILL WORKED at the adventure travel company where I had been employed before Ralph's accident, pulled me aside one day when she came for a visit. "How are you doing?" she asked, looking earnestly into my face. "I mean, really, how are you?"

"Okay," I said. It was my standard answer.

"Well, you know, Suzy, I've gotta tell you, I think Ralph is doing remarkably well. You know, don't you, that when we all heard at work about his accident, we were worried. Not just whether he would survive, but also how he would cope. No one could remember a single time when Ralph had ever asked for help with anything. We didn't know how he'd get by, dependent on others."

It was true. Ralph never requested favors or assistance from anyone. It was the other way around. When someone needed to borrow a tool or a specific type of athletic gear, it was Ralph who usually had it. If anyone had a mathematical problem they could not solve, they called Ralph. If they needed a place to spend the night or a ride to the mountains, they could usually count on us.

Although he complained about mysterious pain in his legs

and arms and about not being able to find a comfortable position in his wheelchair, Ralph didn't dwell on why the accident had happened to him. Sometimes he'd simply say, "It was just dumb luck."

Rachel was right. He was doing amazingly well for someone who had once been the most independent person I knew. I was the one who was falling apart.

Chapter 22

Baby Jane

In some perverse state of mind I rented and watched the movie *Whatever Happened to Baby Jane?* I stayed up late one night drinking gin-and-tonics and wondering if I was, as I suspected, a reincarnation of Baby Jane as played by Bette Davis. I suspected that I had begun to resemble Baby Jane in her most frenzied, hysterical state.

Ralph watched an old Marx Brothers black-and-white comedy in the other room. He refused to view what he considered a silly movie about a washed-up, wheelchair-bound movie star trapped inside her house by a demonic sibling.

But I was fascinated. I had seen the movie once or twice before on late-night television, but that was prior to our life becoming such a train wreck; B.R.A., I called it—Before Ralph's Accident.

I recognized and identified with poor Baby Jane's two-faced response to her sister's (the forever-suffering Joan Crawford) condition. One minute Baby Jane was kind. The next she was manic. Then she was downright cruel, demented, and manipulative. Next she flipped into remorsefulness. She was contrite, wanting only to give love and receive it in return.

But the worst parts of the movie for me were the look in

Baby Jane's eyes after she had done something particularly heinous to her sister. I looked at my own eyes in the mirror. I concluded that I had not turned into Baby Jane just yet. But I was getting close.

∽∾

Mrs. Scott recognized my Baby Jane potential and tried to keep me stable. She constantly recommended that I rest, that I put my feet up on a chair and relax, that I lie down and take a nap.

One day, she came over and looked at me carefully, as if I was a scientific experiment.

"Baby, you don't look so good. What's wrong? Let me see your face."

I turned from the dishes in the sink and stared into her brown eyes.

"Lord have mercy!" she exclaimed. "You need to lay down right now! We need to rub your body up and down with green alcohol and then we need to cover you with lotion!"

She leaned in closer and studied me. "I'm worried about you," she whispered. "You're always runnin'. You need to slow down, sweetheart, before you pop a brain cell or somethin'."

She got up off the stool she had been sitting on and searched inside my kitchen cupboards. "You got any bourbon around here? A hot toddy is what you need. Squeeze in a little lemon. Chop up some onion. Drop in a spoon full of honey. It'll put a smile on your face that will light up this room."

She found an old bottle of Jim Beam, unscrewed the top, and smelled it. She smiled. "I know what I'll do. I'll make us both one right now. I'm feelin' kinda under the weather myself. Get me two glasses, a lemon, an onion, and some honey. Hand me a knife." I slipped her what she asked for as if I was a scrub nurse in a sterile operating room.

"My daddy used to call this his exlixer," she said. "It'll fix anything."

She poured two generous shots into the glasses, squeezed half a lemon in each, threw in a big dollop of honey, and added a tiny bit of tap water.

"We don't have time to fire up the stove or chop that onion. We can drink another one later if we need to. We've got to get us the cure right now." Mrs. Scott handed me a glass and clinked hers with mine. "Bottoms up, sugar."

I watched Mrs. Scott gulp down her drink and get ready to make another. I wondered if Baby Jane drank exlixers before she turned mean or after she was nice, but I didn't have time to dwell on the question because Mrs. Scott had begun to sing as she chopped an onion. *"This'll cure what ails us, oh yeah . . . this'll chase our blues away, oh yeah . . ."*

Chapter 23

EXPLORING THE NEIGHBORHOOD

AFTER RALPH BROKE HIS neck and we had to give up our plan to move to Crested Butte, I felt we had no choice but to stay in North Oakland. Nowhere else could we find better care for Ralph, I told myself. No place in the United States had a population as tolerant and knowledgeable about disabilities. Look at all the cultural activities, the opportunities, the other disabled people living meaningful, enriched lives in and around nearby Berkeley. I heard myself telling others that the Bay Area was the best place on earth to be if you were in a wheelchair.

And it was true, even if every block did not have a curb cut and sometimes there was no way for Ralph to cross the street. There were many restaurants, bookstores, and movie theaters that were completely inaccessible. Still, it was better than Podunk, Minnesota; Tulsa, Oklahoma; Anchorage, Alaska; or Philadelphia, Pennsylvania.

But the reality was that we weren't able to leave the Bay Area because we couldn't leave behind our debts or our HMO. Real estate values had gone down, so we couldn't sell our two-story house and get something more wheelchair-friendly.

Ralph's first night at Highland General Hospital had cost

nineteen thousand dollars. One bottle of Valium cost eighty dollars. Two bottles of Zoloft sold for one hundred. Although insurance had covered most of these expenses, we'd developed some very costly habits that had followed us home.

We lived in what creative real estate agents called lower, lower Rockridge. To some, lower, lower Rockridge was located on the wrong side of the freeway, the bad side of Shattuck Avenue, but the good side of Martin Luther King Jr. Way.

After Ralph's accident, I spent serious time getting to know our neighborhood. I volunteered to deliver the community newsletter. My delivery area encompassed six square blocks. That was fine with me. It was about all I could handle.

Within the quadrant were three small churches—one Pentecostal and two Baptist—one liquor store, one low-income apartment complex, and, to my knowledge, no crack houses. Several of my neighbors ran businesses out of their homes: a licensed daycare provider, a tax expert, a hairdresser, and an entrepreneur who sold sexy women's underwear.

Most of the houses on my block were owned by black couples who had raised their children on these quiet streets. Some of those children still lived with them, as did grandchildren and great-grandchildren.

There were many little kids and plenty of dogs, a wild green parrot that nested in my neighbor's tree, and a rabbit that often escaped from its cage around the corner and came into our garden. We had hummingbirds and butterflies, numerous squirrels, a possum, and possibly two raccoons. The Jamaicans who lived across the street wore their hair in dreadlocks and kept Christmas lights up year-round.

Ours was not the only house with a wheelchair ramp. Mr. Washington used a walker, Miz Lola had two hearing aids, Ida

Jones was blind, Mr. Smith smoked cigarettes while breathing through tubes that were hooked to an oxygen tank.

The most ostentatious thing within the six square blocks was Mr. Fontenot's mint-condition turquoise 1959 Cadillac. It took up his entire driveway, and still the fins stuck out over the sidewalk. He never drove it, but he hired Jerry to wash and wax it monthly.

Jerry coveted that car. He said the paint job wasn't turquoise. He said it was money green.

Chapter 24

A Walk on the Wild Side

I FINALLY CONVINCED JERRY to exercise. He rose early one morning before Ralph was awake, put on a pair of white shorts, a white muscle T, white athletic socks, and very clean white sneakers. He came downstairs and announced, "I'm ready for that walk."

We went outside into the bright sunlight. "Lord, it's hot out here." Jerry squinted directly into the morning sun.

We walked up Dover Street toward Alcatraz Avenue. Jerry offered a running commentary as we meandered along the sidewalk.

"Looka that yard. Now don't that look good? That's what I like." He pointed at a perfectly tended, tiny lawn, one where, on a previous walk, I had seen a hunched, ancient man cutting blades of grass with a pair of manicure scissors.

A bit farther up the street, we came to a yard filled with white pebbles. A few mangy rosebushes dotted the stone-covered plot. "Now that's what I like," said Jerry, "even better then the place with grass. Not much upkeep on this yard. No sir, that's what I like."

We continued on our way. We stopped in front of a small yard completely covered in Astro Turf. "Wait," shouted Jerry. "I take that back. This here is my favorite yard. Yessir. Specially when it's new like this and really green. No upkeep, no sirree. That's what I like!"

Oh my God, I thought to myself as we walked on.

At the end of Dover Street, where it ran into Alcatraz, a small dilapidated house sat on the corner, with no yard whatsoever. The entire area in front of the house was paved in cement. Three cars were squeezed next to one another, parked in a space meant for two. One of the cars was a shiny black BMW, another was a restored Datsun 240Z, and the third was a new tawny-colored Lexus.

"Oh, Momma, mmmm-mmmmm," Jerry sang. "Now here is the yard I really like."

Chapter 25

HARKA

HARKA ARRIVED AT OUR house at the end of February. He'd packed a little plastic valise and walked three days to a bus stop on a desolate mountain road in Nepal. When the bus came, he'd sat in the front seat and hadn't moved for another eleven hours. His bus journey ended in Katmandu. He stayed at a friend's apartment for the night, then took another bus to the Katmandu International Airport. There he boarded a jet airliner and flew sixteen hours to America.

Our friends Laurie and Betsy met him at SFO. They took him directly to Andronico's on University Avenue in Berkeley so he could see an American grocery store. Then Betsy took him back to her house, where he fell asleep.

At 6 P.M. that same day, Betsy woke Harka and took him to dinner at an Indian restaurant on Shattuck Avenue. That's where Ralph and I met him.

Harka had been Betsy and Laurie's guide on numerous treks in Nepal. They had sponsored his trip to the United States by completing the paperwork, putting up some of the funds, and guaranteeing his character to the authorities.

He arrived wearing a blue cotton sweat suit and flip-flops. In his plastic valise were a dress shirt and pants, a pair of black socks and shoes, and the addresses and phone numbers of forty-five people to contact who were friends of friends of friends who had gone trekking with Harka and his fellow guides.

Laurie and Betsy had asked Ralph and me if Harka could stay with us. They thought we could use an extra pair of hands.

It sounded good to us. We agreed immediately. At dinner that night, they asked Harka how he felt about the plan. "Very fine," he said, nodding. "Very fine, indeed."

But, it wasn't clear whether he'd understood a word they said. He seemed the most agreeable person on earth.

After leaving a small Nepalese village with no running water or electricity, and wallowing in mud and water buffalo turds from his father's herd, Harka probably didn't consider hanging around our house that bad. After dinner, we brought him home.

"Here is your room," I said, showing him the unoccupied back bedroom. It was a room I had tried to sleep in after Ralph's accident, before I had found myself wandering from bed to bed and sofa to sofa in the middle of the night.

"Very nice," said Harka, smiling. I could tell he was delighted.

"Sweet dreams," I said, closing the door behind me. "Don't let the bedbugs bite."

"What is it that you say?" asked Harka.

"I'll tell you in the morning. Get some rest. We are very glad that you are here. Namasté."

"Ahhhh, Suzy, very good," answered Harka, placing his palms together and bowing to me. "Namasté to you too. I am very happy, very happy to be here in America."

When I took Harka to the store to buy him a pair of sneakers, he selected cheap basketball shoes. They looked enormous at the ends of his skinny legs and tiny body, and I hoped no one would mug him for his fake designer white-and-black high-tops. But this concept was too complicated to explain to the innocent newcomer.

Harka and I walked to the hospital to pick up Ralph's newest prescription. On a side street, between Shattuck and Telegraph avenues, we passed a homeless woman slumped against the wall of a building. I recognized her as the disoriented drug addict I often saw in the neighborhood. Her face was dirty and bloated. She was missing teeth, and her hair was matted against her forehead. I always gave her a wide berth when I passed by.

Harka stopped in front of her and stared, then followed me slowly, looking back over his shoulder. His face was twisted in pain. He was speechless.

I was speechless, too. How could I explain to him that in a land so plentiful, there were people who were worse off than his countrymen in Nepal?

We continued walking.

A shiny silver Corvette was parked in front of the hospital. Harka gazed at it with curiosity.

"Suzy, what this?" he asked. "Only two people fit in this car?"

"That's right, Harka, it's a sports car and it is very expensive."

"Ah, yes, but only two seats, only two people fit into this car. Why expensive?"

"Because," I said.

"Why?" he repeated.

"Ask Jerry about it when we get home."

"Nice car, Corvette." He rubbed a bony finger on its polished surface. "I like. Maybe some day I get."

❧

Harka had never seen anyone quite so large as Mrs. Scott, and for a long time he seemed frightened by her. He was intimidated by Jerry's size and casualness. He was not accustomed to men walking anywhere without a shirt, even in the tropical areas of Nepal. Jerry's big naked chest, bare feet, and low-slung sweat pants embarrassed him. Harka immediately acquired a collared sports shirt that he tucked into new, perfectly pressed khakis held up by a thick leather belt. He always dressed as if he were going to the golf course instead of coming downstairs to take care of Ralph.

Mrs. Scott would come into the house and greet Harka by picking him up off his feet and squeezing him hard. He looked like an uncomfortable rag doll (dressed for the links) in her massive arms, but in time he grew used to her physical ministrations and even seemed to enjoy them.

Jerry always greeted Mrs. Scott with a big kiss and a shout. "Hey, Momma, how's by you?" Harka called her Mrs. Scottie, as if someone from Star Trek had entered through the back door.

One morning, I walked into the kitchen and overheard Harka, Jerry, and Mrs. Scott in a serious discussion.

"What's going on?" I asked.

"Harka here is telling us about the caste system over in Nepal," said Mrs. Scott. "Jerry and I know all about that, don't we?"

"Yeah boy," said Jerry, shaking his head.

"What do you know about it?" I asked.

Mrs. Scott stared at me. "You don't know nothin', do you? Nothin' about life at all."

"I heard that," seconded Jerry.

Chapter 26

Finding Out About Jerry

It DIDN'T TAKE ME long to figure out Jerry's biggest vice, but it took me a while to accept his nocturnal habits.

Every payday, he borrowed the van, stayed out all night, gambled away his paycheck, and came home broke, smelling of cigarettes, fried onions, and something that had gone bad in the garbage. Then he borrowed on his next paycheck, until there was enough to spend only one night out a week.

This system worked well for an attendant and his charge. Too broke to go anywhere, Jerry was always available for Ralph's needs and mine, except for payday night.

I learned to adapt. I didn't know where Jerry went or whom he was with or what he did when he was with them, but I was willing to compromise. After all, I was learning to adjust to Ralph's disability and the world's reaction to it. What was one night alone?

One early morning around 3 A.M., though, Jerry came home and asked me for money. When I told him I didn't have any, he continued to stare at me.

"Nothin'? You sure you ain't got somethin' somewhere?" He was close to pleading.

I took out all my coats and jackets, jeans and pants and

scraped around in the pockets. I crawled under the bed and searched behind bureaus and between couch cushions. I emptied every piggy bank and junk depository in the house. I came up with four dollars and seventy-four cents. He took it. He went out into the cold, foggy Oakland night. I never asked him what happened and he didn't tell me.

∽o∾

Jerry brought home a big bag of chicken thighs one day and asked Ralph if he wanted to buy them from him.

Ralph thought for a moment and said, "No."

Mrs. Scott was in the kitchen cooking greens. "Shit," she mumbled, "ain't nobody gonna buy them chickens from you. Ain't fresh. No tellin' where they been. Better price at the Pac n' Save and they be fresh."

Jerry took the thighs away.

The next week Jerry brought home a baby blue leather suit. When I came home from work and saw it draped over the chair, I knew it was for me. It had zippers, pockets, and epaulets, and a quilted removable lining. The pants looked as if they might squeeze the hips and thighs of an anorexic sixteen-year-old, and the legs flared into bells. All I needed was eight-inch platform heels and an Afro.

"Jerry," I said, "I'm sorry, but I don't have the hairdo or the shoes or anywhere to go in this get-up. I don't need this suit."

"Baby," Jerry said in his smoothest, sexiest voice, "this suit will look good on you. Match those pretty blue eyes. Hug those thighs of yours."

"Jerry, did you win this suit in a card game, steal it, or what? Do you want me to buy this suit from you?"

We stared at each other for a moment.

Jerry took the fully lined, bell bottomed, pocketed, epauletted, zippered, baby blue, calf-leather suit away. I never saw it, or the chicken thighs, again.

∽o∾

It was 4 A.M., feeding time. I was awakened by the sound of sucking, chewing, and belching. Loose cereal shaking against a box, spoon clanging against Fiestaware.

Jerry was eating again. Sometimes it was Frosted Flakes, other times it was Froot Loops. I bought big bags of sweet cereal at Pac n' Save just for Jerry. He was very appreciative. In the wee hours of the morning, he sat naked on the edge of his bed and ate as if he had been stranded on a deserted island, starving to death.

I could just make out his broad bare back hunched over the cereal bowl as he chowed down. When he was finished, he rolled back into bed and put his arms around me. "Come on," he said. "It's chattin' time, baby."

"Whaddya wanna talk about?" I yawned and stretched and cuddled up against his smooth body.

"You," he whispered. His voice was deep and raspy.

"No," I said, "you tell me a story. Like how'd you get that naked lady tattoo on your arm? When did you get it?"

"A long time ago," he answered.

"How long?"

"Oh, baby, I don't know."

"Did you get it in prison?"

No answer. His eyes were closed.

"Have you been to prison?"

"Once," he mumbled.

"When?"

"A million years ago."

I disentangled myself from his arms and propped myself up on my elbows. He turned his back to me.

"Why were you in prison, Jerry?"

He didn't answer. He started to snore. I decided against waking him up. Maybe I didn't really want to know.

∽o∾

I began to obsess about Jerry's secret life. I wanted to know his history. Each week, I got more and more pieces of his past. Sometimes the puzzle parts fit together, and sometimes they didn't.

Early one morning, I awoke to the crunch and smack of Lucky Charms. The glow of the TV lit the room.

"Jerry," I said, staring at his naked back. "I can't figure this out."

"What, baby?"

"If you were married at sixteen and had two babies by the time you were seventeen, how come you didn't graduate from high school until five years later?" I was on to something. The years didn't add up. We'd been back over this often, but tonight I sensed he might be weak and give me some answers. We'd made love earlier, and the sex was getting even better. I couldn't believe how good Jerry made me feel.

I looked around the room where Ralph and I used to sleep. It looked different since Jerry had moved in. There were piles of dirty clothes, mainly sweat shirts and sweat pants that I'd brought home for him from the lost and found at the gym; an old electric typewriter he'd "won" in a card game and said he was going to fix; a black-and-white television perched upon the color one Ralph and I had given him; a broken turntable on the floor; a small refrigerator; piles of wrinkled bills; scraps of paper; shoe boxes full of broken electric razors, flashlight parts, Afro combs, half-empty bottles of hair gel. The stringless guitar was propped against the wall next to the velvet painting depicting a pond surrounded by trees, which Jerry hadn't gotten around to hanging.

On my side of the bed, clothes were piled a foot deep. I'd always had the habit of throwing everything on the floor so I could find it. And lately, drawers had become too difficult.

"Come on, Jerry, explain it to me," I whined. "Something is missing."

He sighed. "Well, baby, I went away."

"You went away? You mean to jail?"

Big sigh. "Uh-huh."

"For what?"

"I don't know, girl, pimpin' and panderin', statutory rape, somethin' like that."

I didn't say anything for a moment. "What happened?" I whispered.

"A little white girl I was messin' with. Turned out she was underage and her being white and all and the judge being white, and it was 1952, '53 . . ."

"Jerry, how'd you meet her?"

"I can't remember that, baby. She was into us black cats. She was a fine little devil and she told the judge she did it 'cause she wanted to, but that's all that ol' white judge wanted to hear and he sent me up the river, made an example of me, you know?"

"Where'd he send you?"

"San Quentin, darlin'. Five years."

"Were you scared?"

"Shit, yeah, I was scared. Scared to death. Everybody told me to keep my back to the wall, don't turn round in front of nobody, and don't bend over to pick up soap in the shower."

"Did anything bad happen when you got there?"

Jerry tossed the empty cereal box across the room, into the trash can. He slid under the covers, propped his cheek on his right hand, draped his left arm across my waist, and looked at me.

"You know, that's the funny thing 'bout it. I got to prison and I knew everybody there. Everybody I thought was dead or in the army was in San Quentin. And everybody was glad to see me. Wanted to know what was goin' down on the streets and who was fuckin' who. It was like homecomin' or somethin'. Guys who worked in the kitchen bringing me extra sandwiches and guys who worked in the laundry starching my clothes so I looked real sharp. I was almost a big shot in San Quentin."

"What happened after that wore off?"

"Didn't wear off, baby. I was a big shot everywhere I went. Next they shipped me to Tracy and that was like a country club. I was a big shot there, too. Worked in the slaughterhouse, learned to play the horn, stayed outta the war, went to school. Know'd everybody there and kept outta trouble. Toed the line, and when I got back out I was alive. Everybody else left out on the streets was dead. Prison, it saved my life, baby. It was the best thing that ever happen to me, really. Saved my ass, that's for damn sure."

∽o∾

It was another payday and, according to Ralph, Jerry owed him fifty-two dollars and eighty-five cents. Jerry borrowed another twenty dollars and went out.

At 3:23 A.M., the sound of someone munching dry cereal woke me up.

"What's going on?" I whispered.

"Eatin'," he replied. "And you know, I don't know how I can owe Ralph so much money. It don't make no sense."

"Maybe you need to get a second job."

"A second job so I can afford to work the first job, 'cause I don't make enough money at the first job to pay off what I owe for the first job. Just don't make no sense, does it?"

"Guess not. Maybe you could take those cans you're saving down to the recycling place and get some money. I'm sick of that trash in the backyard."

"Okay, baby, but you know, I had a dream last night that Ralph was riding a horse and chasin' me, throwing IOUs at me."

"Well, don't worry about it. How much do you think you owe me?"

"Girl, I owe you everything. I owe you my life."

"Good. That's what I wanted to hear. Now go to sleep. I'll take care of you."

He rolled over. I snuggled up against his warm, smooth body.

"You know, girl," Jerry whispered in my ear, "we were meant to be together."

"Jerry, I don't think so."

"Oh yeah, girl, I woulda found you."

"Jerry, before Ralph's accident, if you had been walking toward me on the sidewalk, I would have crossed the street to walk on the other side. I would have been scared of you. My mother and father raised me to stay away from men like you."

"Baby, I woulda found you," Jerry said with the certainty of Buddha.

Chapter 27

STRANGE PLACES

I'VE BEEN TO EUROPE, Africa, Asia, and Central America. I've traveled north to Alaska and south to Tasmania. I've stayed in smelly Mexican campgrounds, snowbound Himalayan huts, rat-infested apartments, and a grand old hotel along Lake Geneva in pristine Switzerland. But the strangest place I ever visited is two doors down from my house at Mrs. Scott's home.

Her palace is a small shotgun apartment. You walk up three steps onto the porch, step through the front door, and are immediately in the living room. Beyond is the kitchen; down the dark hallway, past the bathroom, is her bedroom. How she has the apartment decorated and organized is a mystery to me.

Piled high against the living room walls are boxes of unused supplies she's bought on sale at Pac n' Save. There's no place to sit on the couch because it's covered with dishtowels and plastic bags full of children's clothes. In the same room sits a long portable rack on which hangs a black-velvet evening gown, Hawaiian shirts, rhinestone decorated sweaters, and several pink lacy nightgowns. The rack is on wheels but can't be moved because it's surrounded by cardboard cartons filled with scraps of material, tattered papers, bits of ribbon, buttons, bottle caps, and other treasures. Mrs. Scott has carved a narrow path through her belongings, just big enough for her large body to squeeze through.

"Mrs. Scott," I say, as I glance over her possessions while following her into the kitchen. "Isn't that my potholder over there by the mirror?"

"Why yes it is, darlin'," she answers without looking. "And you can have it back any ol' time you want." But I realize that reaching it is impossible, and besides, I don't seem to need it as much as Mrs. Scott appears to.

We step into her kitchen, which is cramped and cluttered. Her cupboards overflow so that she can't close the doors. Bottles of vinegar, cans of black olives, jars of yellow mustard and sweet pickles spill from the shelves. Lined up on the countertops are unopened boxes of cereal, crackers, and cookies. Nearby are big bags of pinto beans, rice, cake flour, oatmeal, and potatoes. It is as if she's preparing for the end of the world.

There is a small, round Formica table on which sits a medium-sized lamp with fluted shade, a china sugar bowl shaped like a cow, and plastic salt and pepper shakers. Two high-backed aluminum chairs with brown Naugahyde cushions, tucked under the table, are the only places in the apartment to sit, except for the purple fur-covered toilet seat and Mrs. Scott's bed.

Scattered across the linoleum floor are metal buckets filled with rags, sponges, and cleaning supplies. Perhaps, I think, she plans to straighten up before Armageddon.

"You need any green alcohol?" Mrs. Scott shouts, pointing to a case in the corner. "Here, take some," she says before I can answer, pressing two plastic bottles at me. "You need it, I'm sure."

Down the hallway, past the refrigerator, I peek inside the bathroom and see more clothes hung from a bent shower curtain rod, orange bottles of pills on the windowsill, and a pyramid of toilet paper stacked on the floor. Then it's on to Mrs. Scott's boudoir, with its king-size bed covered in multicolored pillows and handmade quilts. A glass vanity table can be reached only by traversing Mrs. Scott's mattress. An ancient black-and-white television, with rabbit-eared antennae, sits on a crowded bureau. I must crawl across Mrs. Scott's blankets and pillows in order to change the channels.

When I walk through Mrs. Scott's apartment, I do so with caution, afraid something might fall on my head. But, at the end of each visit, I have to drag myself outside. I want to take off my shoes and socks, stretch out in Mrs. Scott's soft, comfortable bed, hide beneath her thick, warm comforters, and go to sleep for a very, very long time.

Chapter 28

CAPTAIN SCOTT

WHILE I WAS TRYING to piece Jerry's life together, I was also working on Mrs. Scott's.

I knew that she was the youngest of twelve children, all of them raised in East Texas. Her daddy was a preacher. Her momma was part Cherokee. Mrs. Scott told me she sang gospel with her sisters throughout the South. Known as the Hall Sisters, they performed before and after her daddy's sermons.

We sat in her cramped apartment one day and squinted at a fuzzy black-and-white photo she pulled from a drawer. She said it was a picture of her family's house. In the foreground was a scrawny hound dog. Behind the squatting dog was Mrs. Scott's daddy from the knees down, and behind him was a shack on cinder blocks set in the dirt.

"That's my daddy there, Suzy Parker, and that's his old dog, Jack, and behind them, well, that's the ranch house, the Hall Estate. Lord have mercy, there were some good times in that house! Lots of food and lots of love."

I squeezed my eyes shut so that I could imagine the Hall Estate with Mrs. Scott's daddy and the loving singing sisters sitting around a big wooden table full of food.

As far as I could tell, Mrs. Scott had been married at least two times. Her first marriage was to her grammar school teacher. She referred to him as "the good one." He was the father of her son, Damian Dewey Hall.

After the good husband died, she took up with Albert, "the bad one."

"Suzy Parker," Mrs. Scott shouted as she sat on a stool in my kitchen, "that man was bad! Woke up one morning and said 'Baby, I'm goin' to Reno to make us some money,' and that was the last I saw of him. Heard he had a wife and eight children up there all the time he was with me. Can't trust a black man, no way, honey. Uhn-uh. Can't trust 'em, that's for sure." Mrs. Scott shook her head in hopeless disgust.

Mrs. Scott said that Elvin Johnstone, "the white one," was the best of her husbands. He was rich, generous, and of German descent. According to Mrs. Scott, he had a little pecker but could "thrill her like no other man." I gathered that Mrs. Scott had been domestic help for Mr. Johnstone's ailing wife. When she died, Mr. Johnstone kept Mrs. Scott on as a cleaning lady and that's when things become unclear. At some point, Mrs. Scott went from cleaning lady to lover to caretaker: Mr. Johnstone married her, became ill, and then died in the Oakland fire of 1991.

Mysteriously, there are no pictures of Mr. Johnstone around Mrs. Scott's narrow, stuffy apartment. There are no photographs of any of the husbands, or the son, or the many foster children she says she has raised. There are only big portraits of Mrs. Scott in her "looker" days, a photo of an unsmiling bespectacled black woman with Indian features, and the picture of Jack the dog and Mrs. Scott's daddy below the knees on the family estate.

On a visit from East Texas, Mrs. Scott's son, Damian, told me his mother once broke the arm of a man who was rude. He said that she had thrown another man over the back fence after he had acted "dumb."

Mrs. Scott said that one night she heard a burglar in her apartment. She rolled out of bed, heated some oil in a frying pan, threw the hot oil in the face of the intruder, hit him over the head with the skillet, wrestled him to the floor, hauled him to the front door, and tossed him into the street. He never came back.

Mrs. Scott assured me that as long as she was my friend, I didn't have much to worry about. I'd be safe in my own neighborhood with Mrs. Scott living down the street, looking after me. "Sweetheart, you don't need nobody but me," Mrs. Scott shouted. "Just let me know what you need, Suzy Parker. Momma Scott is here for you, sugar. She's here."

✥

One day, when Mrs. Scott and I were at the hospital, waiting for Ralph's appointment to end, I decided to clean out my purse. As I piled junk high on the seat between us, Mrs. Scott picked up my address book and thumbed through it.

"Look here, Suzy Parker. Half these people you don't hear from no more. You ought to cross out their names and put down your real friends. Give me somethin' to write with."

I gave her a pen. She turned to the letter S and wrote in her big cursive hand her name, address, and phone number. Then she turned the page over and wrote the identical information on the back of the S page.

She continued to study the address book while I flipped through a magazine. It wasn't until a few days later, when I was looking up someone's number, that I noticed that Mrs. Scott had made several entries between the addresses and phone numbers. Under one old friend's name, she had written, *Get rid* of him, *he's no good!* and under another name, she had scrawled, *Old friend we don't hear from no more.* By a third name, she wrote, *He's nice. Invite him for dinner.* And beside her own name, on each side of the letter **S** page, she had written, *Truly yours, your best friend, Mrs. Gerstine Scott.*

Chapter 29

BIG PROBLEMS IN LITTLE CITY

ONE OF HARKA'S NEPALI friends took him to Reno to gamble. Harka was transformed. He bought lottery tickets every week and watched the news to see if he had won. When the lottery got so big in New Jersey that it was about to burst, Harka begged me to call my brother Bill in Atlantic City and ask him to buy tickets for us. "I will share my prize money," he said solemnly. "I promise."

He began taking the bus alone to Reno on his days off. He called us once in the middle of the night to say that he'd missed the casino-to-Oakland shuttle but we shouldn't worry, he'd catch the next one.

He arrived home in the morning, sleepy but euphoric.

"What happened?" we asked.

"Oh, many problems. Many, many big problems. Very bad. But I fix, you know?"

"What did you fix?"

"Three guys," he said, showing us three fingers. "I meet three guys in trouble."

"Yes?" said Ralph

"From Korea, you know? Three guys from Korea."

"Go on," I said.

"They need my help. Bus not come, you know? Bus not come and three guys who lose big money from Korea, they not know what to do."

He paused and looked at us so that the seriousness of this situation could sink in.

"These three guys," he continued. "From Korea. They lose big money and bus not come. They look at me. They point to their watches. *Big watches.* They say 'Bus, bus, bus. Oakland, Oakland, Oakland. Tomorrow Korea.' " He pointed at his own big watch and shook his head.

"I know what they mean, you know? I know bus not come. I know they lose money *big*. I know they need to catch bus to Oakland now because they go to Korea next day. I thinking, thinking, thinking, and I know."

He pointed to his head and nodded. We got the mental picture of Harka thinking.

"I say to them, 'Follow me.' I think Greyhound. But I say, 'Follow me' because I know they not understand Greyhound, but I do and they follow me and we go to Greyhound station, and I go to counter and find out about bus for Oakland. I say to them, 'Bus leave soon. Thirty-five dollars.' The three guys from Korea say, 'Money no problem. Bus not come *big problem*. Plane tomorrow.' "

"Come on," said Jerry. "Get to the point."

"I said, 'Bus leave soon.' They give me money. Oh so much money. I buy ticket. For them. They say 'Thank you. Thank you. Thank you.' I say 'No problem.' Because you know, their English, it is very bad, and I know I say something else, they not understand. Three guys from Korea. Lose big. But they not know English. Not like me. I help them. And they are happy. Oh so happy. They want to buy me drink. They want to give me money. But I say, 'No, this is America. I help you. Someday you

help me. Maybe I come to Korea. Win big. You help me then.'
And they say, 'Yes. You come. We show you very good time.' "

"Did they catch the bus?" asked Mrs. Scott.

"Yes, they catch bus. They very grateful. I am very happy that
I can help them, you know? Because I help them, maybe someday they help me. Or somebody else help me when I miss the
bus. Oh, the bus. It is very bad. It never come on time. Never.
And how come? This is America. The bus should come on
time."

"You know that's the truth," grumbled Mrs. Scott.

Yes, I thought, the bus should come on time. Especially for
Harka, who is so able and willing to help the strangers from
Korea. Ralph, Jerry, Mrs. Scott, and I knew that it was really not
a coincidence that of all the people in Reno, the biggest little
city in America, the three lost men from Korea had turned to
Harka for help.

Chapter 30

THE GOUCH

Mrs. Scott had the gouch. "It's gout," I shouted into her good ear as we sat on her front stoop in the early morning sun.

"I know, baby. That's what I said. I got the gouch." She looked at me as if to say "Don't you know nothin?" but instead explained to me, and anyone within earshot, the symptoms of her malady.

"It's when your feet swell way up and you can't walk. It's from good eatin' and rich livin'. And, ooooooh baby, you know I like to live good." She paused and smiled at me. Then she looked sad. "But it hurts, baby. It hurts awful bad."

Mrs. Scott and I looked down at her swollen toes. It was difficult for me to tell which foot had the gouch. They both looked enormous. But her toenails were painted bright pink and they were peeking out from the tips of her brown Birkenstocks. Mrs. Scott is not one to fall apart, even in the face of enlarged feet and unbearable pain.

I am not unfamiliar with gouch. My mother has it and can barely squeeze into her golf shoes. My father had it and had to wear tennies with his tux at my brother's wedding. His dress shoes just didn't fit.

I'll probably get it myself. Gouch is universal. It's a weak but familial link between Mrs. Scott and myself.

Later in the day, I took Mrs. Scott to a foot clinic in downtown Oakland. A white-coated podiatrist examined her bloated appendages and recommended that she see a medical doctor. The problem was internal not external, he said.

"Oh Lordy, baby," shouted Mrs. Scott, limping out of the office. "You know I've got good feet. That's because I bathe every day. I clean my feet, wash between my toes, and clip my nails. Other people don't do that, you know, sugar? They let their feet get all funky. Their toenails turn black and they hang down like dead crawfish. But not me, baby. I am clean!" She banged her wooden cane for emphasis on the pavement in front of my car. The image of someone's toenails looking like dead crawfish stuck in my throat. I tried not to think of other people's feet.

Mrs. Scott continued her lecture as I helped her into the passenger seat. "Doctor says I should walk, baby, so let's go. He says I need to eat healthy food, like I always do. No sweets. Not much fat. No alcohol, ice cream, or candy. All the good stuff. Gone." She shook her head, which was wrapped in a colorful cotton scarf.

Mrs. Scott looked to me for a response. Then she leaned in real close, her big face peering into mine.

"Baby, growin' old is hell," she said softly. "You know that, don't you?" Then her voice gathered fervor. "But you only come around once in this world, so you've got to make the best of it. You hear what I'm sayin', girl? You got to live right and eat right and do right by other people. Share and be kind and help those less fortunate than yourself. That's what this life is all about.

"Now let's go to Pac n' Save. You got any money? We got to

keep our iceboxes and kitchen cabinets full. Ain't no tellin' what might happen. Here today, gone tomorrow. This here gouch I got is bad, but you know, there are always worse things that could happen. Keep yourself clean and be sweet, Suzy Parker. Live good and share. That's what you've been set down on this earth for!

"Come on now, baby doll, let's go! We got things to do! Help me with this here seat belt, will you? Lord, they just don't make these things big enough, do they?"

Chapter 31

FAMILY

AT THE SAME TIME I was learning about Mrs. Scott, Jerry, and Harka, I was doing anthropological, sociological, and psychological research on the rest of the world. There seemed to be no predicting how people would react to us now.

Some old friends couldn't come in the house. Ricky had to stay out on the back porch. He couldn't bear to see Ralph in that chair. One climber from the gym couldn't get past the kitchen. Ralph's accident was just too much for him. His wife, Kate, cried every time she saw us. Our friend Jake's voice grew soft and sing-songy when he was around us. Leslie opted to drop us altogether.

At public functions, strangers came up to Ralph and introduced themselves. Others stood back, stared, and, when they thought we weren't looking, shook their heads in pity. Many people ignored us.

But the most interesting reactions were from my own family.

I had always felt closer to my mother's side because Aunt Arlene's family had lived nearby and we'd spent summers together at my grandparents' beach house. After the accident, I expected to hear from Arlene's kids, Aunt Mary's kids, and Aunt Rhonda's children. And I did, in one way or other.

But it was my father's side of the family that really kicked in. For months, they sent us checks, letters, presents, and words of encouragement. We received phone calls, poems, inspirational books, and photographs of their extended families. I heard from every female cousin on my dad's side of the family many times, and his sisters and their husbands—who were growing old and sick themselves—kept up with us on a regular basis.

The only explanation seemed to be that my father's side of the family had felt more pain than my mother's. My mother had grown up in a sprawling suburban home with a big back-yard and a tennis court. My dad and his two sisters lived in a comfortable but cramped bungalow, on the other side of the tracks. Aunt Jennie became a single mother during the war. Aunt Sophie gave birth to a severely disabled son. Cousin Greg died of cancer at age four; his brother, Joey, was killed in a fatal boating accident; their sister, Tanya, had had a kidney trans-plant. Uncle Wes left Aunt Jennie but not before taking all the towels and sheets with him; cousin Richie developed a nasty drug habit, put on weight, and acquired too many tattoos. Cousin Leah's husband left her and their four kids for his step-mother's daughter; cousin Rob married a cocktail waitress from Jersey City. My father's family had had their share of trou-bles, and maybe that's the reason they didn't flinch from mine.

∽o∾

My cousin Reenie, the dog groomer from Hoboken, called and announced, "It's the Muzzie Curse."

"What are you talking about?" I asked.

"Look, you don't think this stuff that happened to you didn't happen for a reason, do you? Grandma Muzzie cursed us all before she died. That's why Ralph had his accident, Tanya had to have a kidney transplant, cousin Greg died, Josie is mentally retarded, and I'm married to a man who doesn't make enough money."

"Reenie, I don't think so," I replied hesitantly.

"No, really, think about it. Remember how mean she was? Remember how she hated everybody and wouldn't let anyone help her and then got mugged when she was eighty-six years old, then walked seven miles in the rain to the doctor's office with plastic Wonder bread bags wrapped around her feet, and came home and dropped dead? I'm telling you, this family is cursed."

I had to admit Reenie had a point. Grandma Muzzie was meaner than a snake. She married my Jewish grandfather, but didn't allow any of his family into her house because they were Jews. She didn't like Uncle Wes, Uncle George, or any of the Kennedys because they were Catholics. She wasn't fond of my mother because she had married Muzzie's only son. She didn't really like anyone except her own flesh and blood, and even then she felt she'd been betrayed by their poor choices in marriage.

Grandma Muzzie never went to church, but that didn't stop her from disliking anybody who wasn't Protestant.

Maybe Reenie was right. Maybe this messy life I was living was all caused by mean ol' Grandma Muzzie. Maybe none of this was my fault. Maybe she had put the Muzzie Curse on me and I was paying for all the mean things she said and did to Grandpa Katz's family and every non-Protestant she had ever run across. Maybe that explained why Ralph broke his neck.

∽◦∾

After my mother's father died and Grandmother Daniels had triple bypass surgery, Aunt Arlene, recently widowed herself, lived with grandmom in her big house on an inlet in Ocean

City, New Jersey. But when Aunt Arlene started dating Fred, a widowed neighbor who raised orchids, Grandmom Daniels moved in with my parents.

That lasted six months. Grandmom Daniels was too demanding, purposely forgot to put in her hearing aid, and, in most of the family's opinion, drank too much.

My mother and her sisters put Grandmom in a very expensive nursing home against her will. She wanted to live with one of them, but they felt they could not give her the care she needed. She walked slowly with a walker, but for any distance farther than the bathroom, she used a wheelchair. She was too weak to roll the wheels herself, so she had to be pushed—or, in the case of the walker, led wherever she went.

Grandmom hadn't been easy, but she was actually in much better shape physically than Ralph. She could go to the bathroom on her own, dress herself, and put herself to bed at night. She could pour herself a drink, take her medications, and hold her own cards when she played bridge. My mother and her sisters were able to justify putting Grandmom away, but here I was with Ralph.

Visiting my parents after Grandmom had been placed into the nursing home, I found her leopard-print stretch pants in one of the guest room bureau drawers. Grandmom was known for buying very expensive, extravagant clothes. While other grandmothers wore lace blouses, closed at the necks with monogrammed gold brooches, my mother's mother wore plunging necklines and miniskirts well into her eighties. There was a saying in my family that if you went shopping with Grandmom, you should be prepared to spend a lot of money and still look cheap.

I asked my mother if I could have the leopard pants. She said she didn't know. Grandmom was very fussy about her clothes, even the ones she didn't wear. If I didn't ask for permission, we could all be in trouble.

I went down to the nursing home and asked my ninety-six-year-old grandmother if I could borrow her leopard-print stretch pants.

"Hell, yes, you can have them," she said, peering over her thick bifocals. "I can always get another pair if I need to. Now be a good girl and pour your ol' grandmom another drink. And then we've got to figure out a way to get me out of this place."

Chapter 32

MRS. SCOTT'S LESSON

MRS. SCOTT'S URGENT PHONE call woke me at 7 A.M.

"Suze, Miz Buchanan's electricity has been turned off," she bellowed. "We've got to get down to PG&E and pay the bill."

"Okay," I answered groggily. "What time?"

"Nine A.M. sharp. Pick me up." She hung up the phone.

At the appointed hour, I pulled the van in front of her apartment and blew the horn. She lumbered outside, locked her front door, and climbed into the passenger seat. She was out of breath.

"Miz Buchanan didn't have the money to pay the bill," she wheezed. "Now she's sittin' in a funky apartment with no lights. We've got to help her."

"All right," I agreed. "Where does she live?"

"Down on 37th, between Market and Shattuck."

Five minutes later, we pulled in front of a rundown duplex. Mrs. Scott limped to the front door and disappeared inside the dark opening. I slid down in my seat and waited. Ten minutes went by. A loud knock on the window announced her return. I opened the car doors for Mrs. Scott and little Mrs. Buchanan.

"Hello," I said.

Mrs. Buchanan peered at me over her enormous glasses. "Hello, sweetheart. Thanks for comin' by."

The elderly ladies struggled to get in. I had to push Mrs. Buchanan's backside to keep her from falling out the door. She settled primly into the back seat. She wore a long wool coat. Her stockings were rolled to midcalf. On her feet were sturdy brown oxfords, and upon her head she wore a glow-in-the-dark lime green beret. Her large black pocketbook filled her lap.

Mrs. Scott issued orders. "Go down here. Turn right. Now left. Now right again."

Somehow, we arrived at the PG&E building. "Suze, give me twenty dollars," Mrs. Scott demanded. "Miz Buchanan, you come with me. You got that bill now, don't you?"

"Let me see the bill," I said. When the crumpled piece of paper was handed to me, I studied its contents. "This bill is for ninety-eight dollars and forty-four cents. What are we going to do?"

Mrs. Scott answered, "We're gonna give the man twenty dollars. That'll cover it for a while. Then we're gonna cut Miz Buchanan loose. She's gotta take care of her own problems. We've got enough of our own. Wait here."

They climbed out of the van. After thirty minutes, Mrs. Scott thumped the passenger window. I wrestled them back inside the van and waited for my next set of driving instructions.

"Suze, take Miz Buchanan home. We got to get back to your house and take care of Ralph."

I drove to Mrs. Buchanan's apartment and walked her to the front door. We entered a cluttered living room. A dining room table was piled high with newspapers. A half-filled trash bag lay on the floor.

"Mrs. Scott, who lives here with Mrs. Buchanan?" I whispered.

"Nobody, child. Ain't that a shame? Let's go."

"Good-bye," I shouted to Mrs. Buchanan. But it wasn't clear that Mrs. Buchanan understood that we were leaving. She sat on a straight-backed chair and watched us. She still had on her coat. Her glow-in-the-dark lime green beret drooped sadly on her head.

I wondered aloud what would happen when it got dark.

"Nothin' is gonna happen," answered Mrs. Scott. "Just be thankful for what you got, girl. Now let's go home and check on Ralph."

Chapter 33

HOME COOKING

Before the accident, I never went to the grocery store. Ralph did all the shopping because he did all the cooking and because, as with almost everything else, he liked to be in control.

I was happy not to go. But when our world turned upside down and I had to take over that detail, along with everything else, I first tried to pawn it off onto others.

There was no time to go to the store, so I depended on friends to bring us our meals. When they grew tired of shopping for us, I sent the help. I gave them long lists and they sometimes came back with items similar to what I wanted. Brian only went once, forgot half the items on the list, and made the wrong decision about everything else. Vincent, who lived with us for only three weeks, bought the very best of everything, even stopping at the butchers to get fresh fish instead of frozen. Frankie didn't drive, so I left him at home to smoke and drink himself to death. Jerry bought mostly for himself: hot link sausages, pork chops, ground beef, bacon, steak, milk, butter, eggs, Frosted Flakes, Froot Loops, and Wonder bread, three or four loaves at a time.

In order to save money, I started going by myself. Week after week, I bought the same things: three green peppers, two red; a

bag of ready-made salad greens, cheese, eggs, butter; hot links and bacon for Jerry; two gallons of milk; the largest packages of toilet paper and paper towels in the store.

Ralph complained that I was spending too much shopping for everyone else but him. He demanded we go to Costco, a discount warehouse where we could save money.

We piled into the van, Ralph strapped in the back, Mrs. Scott directing from her captain's chair, Jerry at the wheel, and Harka and I across from one another on the wheel wells.

We tumbled out at Costco, got ourselves a sledlike cart and went in. We bought T-shirts and pants for Ralph, a dress for me, pajamas for Harka's mother, giant bottles of artichoke hearts, mighty jars of chopped garlic, four tubes of toothpaste in one package, salon-size containers of shampoo and rinse. When the clerk totaled our bill, it came to over $500. We didn't have a single fresh vegetable or piece of fruit.

We squeezed Ralph into the back of the van, between enormous bags of restaurant-style tortilla chips and gallons of salsa.

Captain Scott smiled and looked at me. "We be cookin' tonight, girl!" she shouted.

∽o∽

Our friends Polly, Steven, and Sandy brought dinner over to our house: Thai take-out and Black Forest cake from Just Desserts bakery.

I set the table. Mrs. Scott arrived and took her place at its head. Jerry and Harka each decided they had something important to do elsewhere.

"What's this?" demanded Mrs. Scott upon seeing the numerous dishes of vegetables, rice, and curry.

"It's Thai food, Mrs. Scott," said Sandy. "I think you'll like it."

"Looks like hay to me."

"Here, let me dish some out for you," said Steven. He heaped Mrs. Scott's plate with several entrees.

"You ain't given this grass to Ralph to eat, are you?" asked Mrs. Scott. "He's a sick man. He needs some meat."

"There is some meat, Mrs. Scott." Polly pointed to the chicken curry smothered in coconut milk.

"Looks like hay to me."

We all looked down at our plates and ate awkwardly, in silence. No one wanted to argue with Mrs. Scott.

But when she mumbled that the food was not fit to eat, Sandy said, "Mrs. Scott, this food was very expensive and it is very good. You should try to be more polite."

Mrs. Scott rose from her chair, looked at me, and said, "Well Suzy, that does it. I'm goin' home now to fix me some pork chops and a chicken. You be careful what you and Ralph eat. He's a sick man and he needs meat. He don't need no hay and grass."

She grabbed her cane and her enormous pocketbook and headed out the back door. For a three-hundred-pounder, she could be very swift on her feet.

∽o∾

Every day, I was learning a new kind of kitchen table wisdom. When we were happy, we were "standin' in high cotton." When we liked something a lot, it was "good enough to slap your gramma." When I tried to sweep the kitchen floor and Jerry was in my way, he said, "Don't you sweep over my feet, girl, and send me to jail." When we talked about the past, we said, "Get on down, back there." We were always saying "I heard that" after we heard something.

When Mrs. Scott's bones started aching, so did mine. When

Jerry's back went out, mine went out, too. When Harka was depressed, everyone but Mrs. Scott got down in the dumps. When Ralph got a cold, we all got colds.

One of Mrs. Scott's friends hired Jerry to fix an old truck. I hired one of Jerry's daughters to work at the gym, paid Mrs. Scott to cook for us, paid Jerry's friend Slim to finish the backyard fence. I hired Lonnie, Mrs. Scott's daughter-in-law, to clean the house. When she moved back to Texas, I hired Carla, one of Mrs. Scott's many foster children, to take her place. When she began asking for money before coming to clean, I let her go. The neighbors hired Jerry to fix a garage door and Harka to pull weeds. Jerry paid Tyrone down the street for a stolen battery, I paid Mrs. Cooper and Mrs. Jefferson to finish a quilt Mrs. Scott had started. I paid Jerry fifteen dollars to take Ralph to the doctor, ten dollars to pick up pills at the pharmacy, five dollars to go to the store and buy milk for himself.

We were a regular cottage industry. We were starting to look alike and act alike, and we were all getting bigger from Mrs. Scott's cooking. Mrs. Scott called me her daughter; my brother John, her son; my parents, Moms and Pops. Jerry called Mrs. Scott Momma; my brother John, brodder-in-law; me, his baby. Everybody else seemed to be his partner or his cousin. Ralph called Mrs. Scott, Scotty; Jerry, "my man." We were getting more and more tangled up, mixed-around, jumbled together. I began to think we were the ultimate experiment in living: the commune of the nineties, the Walden Pond of the twenty-first century, the Hog Farm on Dover Street.

∽∾⌢

When O.J. Simpson was on trial for murdering his wife and a friend of hers, the subject was sensitive at our house.

Mrs. Scott said, "Any white woman who lets a black man beat her deserves everything she gets. Everybody knows black men ain't no good."

"Everybody knows black men don't kill their wives," Jerry said with authority. "They just beat 'em. It's a po-lice conspiracy."

Ralph and I didn't agree, but we knew better than to argue, even if it was our house.

When the verdict came down, Jerry said, "Told you so, black men don't kill their wives. It was the po-lice."

"Praise the Lord," hollered Mrs. Scott. "He works in mysterious ways."

~∽∾∾~

Jerry made red beans and rice. I put the leftovers together in one Tupperware container. When Mrs. Scott and Jerry found out what I'd done, they both had a fit.

"Why are you so stupid, girl? Don't you know you can't put those beans and rice together? Ain't fit to eat now. You sure are stupid."

And nobody, not even Ralph and I, could eat them beans and rice after I had done what I did to them.

Mrs. Scott and Jerry would sit in the kitchen and discuss my ignorance. It wouldn't matter if I was present or not. When Jerry wasn't there, Mrs. Scott would complain to me of his vices, of which there were many. The biggest, of course, was that he was born a black man, which made him "no good." "Everybody knows that," she said.

When Mrs. Scott wasn't around, which wasn't very often, Jerry complained that she was "ignorant." But when she came stomping in the back door, Jerry would bellow, "Well, hello, Momma. How's by you? Don't you look fine today!"

"Really?" Mrs. Scott would ask, fluttering her eyelashes.

She and Jerry would discuss some incident or other in the neighborhood, and I'd try to follow along as best I could. But invariably they would lose me with a low murmur or a high-pitched rupture of laughter, and I'd wonder what they were talking about.

I was trying hard to stay in control of my household, but it was becoming impossible.

୬୦

One day, I made a special cauliflower dish with lots of garlic, lemon, and horseradish. I found the recipe in the food section of the newspaper. COOKING WITH WINTER VEGETABLES FRENCH BISTRO–STYLE, said the headline. Underneath was a black-and-white photo of a cauliflower. The copy stated, *Behold the lowly cauliflower. Just look what you can do with this ugly vegetable!* I looked. It sounded yummy. "I'll make this for dinner," I declared to no one in particular.

I set about assembling the ingredients. There was a cauliflower in the refrigerator. It had a little gray matter on top, but I dusted it off. There was horseradish on the condiment shelf. God only knew how many years it had been there. I opened the lid. It smelled like horseradish.

I found some soft lemons in the vegetable drawer. These will do just fine, I thought. One more day and they would be the color of ripe avocado. I reached deeper into the refrigerator and found a dry, shedding garlic bulb and an onion that was growing green shoots. I made substitutions for what I did not have: milk for cream, blue cheese for Gruyère, red peppers for green.

I deflowered the cauliflower and sautéed the stems with the onion and garlic in olive oil. The kitchen filled with the pungent odors of root vegetables: humus, soil, and a rich dampness that made me want to sing. "*Michelle, ma belle,*" I hummed as I soaked the florets in the lemon juice and then scalded them quickly in boiling salted water. I added the milk and horseradish to the sautéed stems and made a roux, then threw the entire concoction into the Cuisinart and chopped it to a fine lather. "*Che sarà, sarà,*" I shouted, even though it wasn't French. "Just call me Julia Junior."

I layered the florets and cheese into a deep dish and covered the layers with the garlic-onion-stems-horseradish froth. I set it on the table and preheated the oven. Then I went upstairs to make the bed.

I returned to the kitchen ten minutes later to put the casserole in the oven. It wasn't there! I looked in the refrigerator and opened all the cupboard doors and drawers. I searched through the house and peered outside onto the front porch. I went back into the kitchen and threw open the dishwasher. There was the pan, on the bottom rack, upside-down and empty.

I yelled for Jerry. He appeared at the kitchen door. "Where's my cauliflower casserole?" I said accusingly, holding up the empty orange dish.

"You mean that messy thing that was inside that pot you're holdin'?" he asked.

"Yes," I cried.

"I threw it away before it stunk up the whole house," he said, scrunching up his nose. "Whooooo-*weee,* somethin' went bad in there, girl. Musta been in the refrigerator for months. I almost passed out when I chucked it down the sink." He paused and looked at me. "What's wrong?" he asked. "You look upset."

"Jerry," I said, trying to make my voice sound calm. "That was my special French bistro cauliflower dish. I made it for tonight's dinner."

"You've got to be kidding. That thing was dangerous. I saved your life by getting rid of it!"

He turned away, and, as he sauntered back upstairs to his bedroom, I heard him muttering. "Lord, I hate cauliflower. Only French food I know that's worth eatin' is French fries from Jacques in du Box." He sighed. "She don't appreciate anything I do around here. But, *c'est la vie*," he said, shutting the bedroom door softly. "Jacques Cousteau, Brigitte Bardot, and *whatever will be, will be*."

Chapter 34

LOVE CONNECTION

I COULD TELL HARKA was appalled to find out I was sleeping with Jerry. One morning, about a month after he arrived, I got up and ran into him in the hallway outside Jerry's room. He stared at me, trying to figure out where I had just come from. "Hello, Suzy," he mumbled and then went into the bathroom, shut and locked the door, and did not emerge for a very long time. I waited for him to come downstairs so that I could explain the situation to him, although I wasn't sure I could explain it to myself. But Harka avoided me for the rest of the week. When he had to converse with me, he kept his eyes averted, as if just looking at me would cause evil to possess him.

I wanted to explain to him the comfort that Jerry provided, the intimacy I'd been craving—not only for the physicality of a warm snuggle but for the shared banter, the discovery of something new and totally different, the funny stories and absurd laughter, the way Jerry's very existence in our home caused me to think deeply about issues and values I had never before questioned. But I knew that the social system Harka came from would not have allowed such a relationship, and that Harka's deep-seated prejudice against someone darker-complected than he might not be overcome.

But after a while, Harka loosened up. He bought himself a big color television with his first month's earnings and spent hours in his room, lying in his double bed, flipping the channels with his remote control, and watching Jerry Springer, *The Love Connection*, and his favorite show, *Who Wants To Be a Millionaire*.

I noticed that he was studying the personals section in the East Bay *Express*, and when he got his own phone line and cordless telephone, I suspected that he was running an ad and listening to recorded messages from potential female friends. He arranged with Jerry and Ralph to have Friday and Saturday nights off, and on those days he doused himself with a pungent after-shave lotion. Jerry said that Harka was taking another one of his " 'ho' baths." Mrs. Scott thought that he smelled good.

After he acquired a driver's license (an ordeal of epic proportions) and learned to drive (if you could call it that), he would often ask to borrow the car. We knew he had a date when we saw him scrubbing the seats, wiping down the windows, washing the dented fenders, and polishing the old chrome. He tried in vain to remove Jerry's earthy scent from the upholstery and ashtrays, spraying every inch with Lysol and covering the seats with leopard-spotted beach towels he had bought on sale at Macy's.

Months after his arrival, Ralph bought Harka a computer. A friend gave him lessons on Internet access, and late at night I could hear him tapping away on the keyboard. One morning, after a particularly strenuous midnight finger workout, he came downstairs and asked me where Boston was.

"Harka," I warned. "Boston is very far away. It's all the way

across the United States and north of New York City. You aren't
thinking about going there, are you? It's too far."

"Ahhhhh," he said, "north of New York City. Not too far. I
can fly."

"Harka," I said in my best been-there-done-that voice of
authority, "you aren't considering going to Boston to meet
someone, are you? Long distance relationships never work out.
Don't do it. You'll be sorry."

"Do not worry, Suzy." He smiled and pointed to his head. "I
am very smart guy. I not do something stupid. I promise."

We never spoke of his Internet love life again. He never confided in me about women. He kept his private life to himself
and never asked me about mine. I had to accept the fact that
Harka was probably smarter than I when it came to relationships.

Chapter 35

My Parents' Visit

My PARENTS CAME OUT from New Jersey for a visit. Mrs. Scott cooked them special dinners of the same old thing: fried chicken, potato salad, and bread pudding. Jerry made them his remarkable "International Omelet à la Jerie" which he described as a "western omelet, served with Italian sausage and French bread, made by a black man in America." Harka prepared rice and curry. I made us all strong drinks. It was a tense but loving time. My parents bonded with Harka and Jerry, and especially with Mrs. Scott. Before I could stop them, they'd made plans for her to come and visit them back east.

"We'll take you to Atlantic City, so that you can gamble," said my father.

"We'll shop for fur coats," added my mother.

"Whew girl, I will be there!" shouted Mrs. Scott. "Gerstine is goin' to New Jersey! Moms and Pops had better get ready to rock and roll!" She lifted my father up off the floor, and then she twirled him around.

My father pulled me aside later that day. "Listen, Susan," he whispered, "your mother and I want you to know that whatever you decide to do, it's all right with us. We love you. You're in an impossible situation. I can't tell you what to do, but you tell us what we can do for you and we'll do it." He slipped me an envelope. I knew that there was cash inside.

"It's okay, Dad. We'll get by. I don't know what will happen, but we'll be all right."

He stared at me. "We want to do something for Harka and Jerry. What can we buy them? Do they need new TVs or VCRs?"

"I think they've got everything they need, Dad."

"Well, you let me know. Your mother and I like them both. They're family now. And you need them. I'd like to do something for them. We need to keep them happy."

"Yes," I agreed. "I'm doing everything I can to keep them satisfied, probably more than you want to know." I gave my dad a hug and we went back to join the others.

∽◦∾

We decided to take my parents to Inspiration Point in Tilden Park in the Berkeley hills to look at the view. We piled into the van, drove the windy road up to the top, parked in the disabled spot, and backed Ralph out onto the lift and down into the lot.

Ralph put his wheelchair in high gear with the tilt of his chin. With another tilt, he zoomed off across the parking area.

Before we knew it, he had turned a corner too close, lost control of the chair, tipped over, and crashed. The wheelchair lay on its side with Ralph strapped to it, pointing down an embankment. A rock had kept him from sliding farther. It was also the rock he hit his head on before he passed out.

A crowd of hikers had gathered around him. It took six of us to move Ralph and the chair. As we righted the wheelchair, Ralph came to.

A bicyclist shot down the road to a pay phone and called 911. Within a few minutes, a fire truck and ambulance arrived. An EMT asked Ralph his name, birth date, and what day it was. Ralph appeared to be fine, but there was absolutely no way to tell if he had broken anything below his shoulders. My father took a stick and cleaned dog shit out from between the armrest and the wheelchair's frame.

The firemen and the ambulance crew discussed the options with us. They could unstrap Ralph, put him on a gurney, and take him to the hospital, or we could leave him in the wheelchair and I could take him to the emergency room in our van.

We opted for taking him in the van, because extracting him from the chair was difficult and time-consuming, and the ambulance staff clearly didn't want to deal with it. If something was broken, they didn't want to make it worse by putting him on the gurney.

I drove us all cautiously to the hospital. We checked into the emergency room and began our wait. Four hours went by before we saw a doctor. Ralph couldn't feel anything, so blood tests, X rays, and a CAT scan were taken to find out if anything was wrong.

My parents took a cab home and went to bed. Hours later, the tests came back negative. We made an appointment for an MRI the next day.

I helped the orderlies put Ralph's clothes back on, assisted them in getting him back in the chair, took him out to the van, put him in, strapped him down, and drove home. It was two in the morning.

Jerry got up and helped me take Ralph out of the wheelchair, put him into bed, catheterize him, wash him, brush his teeth, and floss between his molars. Before I turned out the lights I leaned down and whispered into Ralph's ear, "If you do this to me again, Ralph, I will leave you."

I turned away from him before he could answer, hit the lights, and shuffled upstairs to the spare couch, to sleep alone, while my parents shared the guest room.

Chapter 36

Mrs. Scott's Adventure

My mother called me. "Listen, Susan, your father has just spoken with Mrs. Scott on the telephone and they've made arrangements for her to come and visit New Jersey. We'll arrange it so that it's not at a time when you're coming."

"Mom, I don't think you and Dad can handle Mrs. Scott alone. I'll have to be there."

"But then coming to visit us won't be a vacation for you."

"Mom, believe me, you don't want to be left alone with Mrs. Scott. She's too big for you."

"Are you sure?"

"Yes, unfortunately, I am sure. And you do know, don't you, that you'll have to pay for her ticket?"

"No, I hadn't thought of that."

"Oh yeah, too late now. She's comin' and you're payin'."

"Well, I'd better tell your father."

"You do that, Mom. And stock up on ham hocks."

∽∘∾

Mrs. Scott arrived at the Philadelphia International Airport two days after I did. She claimed to have been on an "air-o-plane" before, but I doubted it. Dressed in sequins and glitter, black velvet, faux pearls, and six-carat gold everywhere, she was beside herself with excitement.

My parents and I took her directly from the airport to Ponzio's Diner. We always went to Ponzio's when guests arrived at the airport. But the built-in booths at the diner did not leave enough space between the seat and the table for Mrs. Scott's belly. Although she gave it her best effort, she couldn't squeeze in. The four of us moved to a table for eight, which gave Mrs. Scott more room.

My mother didn't know it, but a surprise seventieth-birthday party was planned for her the following evening at a country club. For the party, Mrs. Scott had made a beautiful quilt. She'd selected the material and the design and was, as always, the director. I had helped with some of the sewing and all of the costs. Mrs. Cooper and Mrs. Jefferson had done the actual quilting. The two of them quilted on a frame in Mrs. Cooper's living room to the accompaniment of a small black-and-white television set, tuned to the daytime soaps and talk shows. All day long, they stitched and stitched, complaining about Mrs. Scott's and my handiwork and shaking their heads at the shenanigans on TV.

Each morning, Mrs. Jefferson had taken a bus to Mrs. Cooper's house. One evening waiting for the bus home, she was mugged on the corner of Martin Luther King and Mac-Arthur. But nothing deterred them from the project. By the time I was ready to leave, it was finished. Mrs. Scott and I had rolled it into a big bundle and stuffed it into a large blue duffel bag. I had brought it on the flight with me.

Mrs. Scott presented it to my mother at the country club. She stood before my parents' friends and families, the lone black woman in a bastion of white conservative Republicans: my father's poker-playing pals; my mother's bridge partners; their golf buddies; old friends from college and high school; even classmates from kindergarten. She sang a gospel tune and gave her standard speech on quilting and the high price of fabric and thread, and then once again, we gently tried to stop her before she took over the rest of the party. She sat back down at the table for the guest of honor, next to my ancient grandmom, and said, "My, my, sister, ain't this some party, or what?"

Grandmom raised up her martini glass, and her gold charm bracelet jingled. "What?" she asked. "I forgot my hearing aid and I can't hear a damn thing. Cheers, Gerstine Scott! Good job."

Chapter 37

PLAGUES

MY GRANDMOM DIED AND I had to go back east for the funeral. I didn't like leaving Ralph home with just Jerry and Harka, but I had no choice. I knew they would take good care of him, but I also knew that Jerry would spend most of his time upstairs in bed and Harka would be in his room, on his computer, searching for a girlfriend.

I'd been in New Jersey less that forty-eight hours when I got a call from Harka.

"Ralph is very sick, Suzy. He is dying. You must come home. He is in hospital and is almost dead."

I tried to calm Harka so that I could find out what was wrong. I gathered that he and Ralph were in the Emergency Room at Kaiser Hospital in Oakland. But that was all the information I could get. I called Jerry at home.

"What's happened to Ralph?" I asked, trying to stay composed. It took Jerry a moment to reply. It was obvious that I had awakened him from a deep sleep. "He's all right," he mumbled. "It's just his leg."

"What about his leg?" I asked.

"There's a bad sore on his foot and it's infected," he said.

"He's down at ER getting fixed, but he'll be okay. Me and Harka can handle it."

I wasn't so sure. I knew that the truth fell somewhere in between Jerry's version and Harka's. Ralph was probably not dying, but he was also probably not doing very well. I knew that I couldn't expect either of them to handle this situation alone.

"I'll call the ER and try to get some information," I said. "I'll also see about flying home early. I'll call you back."

I hung up the telephone and looked at the clock. It was 11 P.M. Eastern Standard Time. My parents and brother were asleep.

I called Kaiser's Emergency Room, and after a thirty-minute wait, I was finally able to speak with someone who had seen Ralph.

"There are complications," said the voice on the other end of the telephone line.

"What are they?"

A throat cleared. "The sore on your husband's heel is deep and causing infection throughout his body. If it's not taken care of, it could mean amputation."

"What?" I whispered.

"We're looking closely at it right now. We have more tests to run and more stabilizing to do. I understand you are out of town. How soon can you get here?"

"I don't know."

"Well, there really isn't any rush. As soon as we can get him a bed, we'll be moving him to the main hospital and turning him over to the orthopedics."

I had been standing up in my parents' living room while I waited on hold, staring absentmindedly out the window. Now I

felt ill. I sat down on the couch. Then I curled into a fetal position with the telephone pressed to my ear.

"Are you still there?" asked the voice.

"Yes," I answered, but I wasn't certain of anything.

"Don't worry," said the voice. "We'll take care of your husband."

"Thank you," I answered, but the line was already dead.

I was shivering, so I went into the guest bedroom and
crawled under the covers, still in my clothes. I lay on my back
and stared at the ceiling. I tried not to think about the foot that
might be amputated, but I couldn't put it out of my mind. I
remembered when all of Ralph's limbs were strong and powerful. His calf and bicep muscles bulged. His blood pumped
rhythmically and efficiently through his cardiovascular system. But now his arms and legs were bloated and unmoving,
stiff, cold, and lifeless, like the limbs of some otherworldly
being. And now someone wanted to cut one of them off.

It's not so bad, I thought to myself. Ralph can't use his legs
or his arms. He doesn't really need them. Maybe it'll make life
easier. He won't have sores to take care of if his heel is gone. He
won't ram into things, stub his toes, and not notice. He will be
lighter, easier to lift and transfer from his bed to his wheelchair
and back again.

But the thought of Ralph disappearing bit by bit was frightening. What would stop the doctors from cutting one foot and
then another, a hand, and elbow, and then a shoulder? There
would be nothing left of my husband.

Another irrational thought came to me. What will the hospital do with Ralph's foot after they cut it off? Where will it go?
Maybe I should ask for it.

I fell asleep and dreamed about Ralph's legs, the ones he had before the accident. They were floating around my head, unattached to his body. Suddenly they swooped down, wrapped themselves around me tightly, and wouldn't let go. They were warm and strong, but they were squeezing the life out of me.

I woke up and looked at the clock. It was 4 P.M. It was time to find my brother and have him drive me to the airport.

✂️∽

The doctors didn't have to cut off Ralph's foot, but they discovered a pulmonary problem that was more worrisome than the sore on his heel. Ralph spent ten days in the hospital. He returned home with his limbs and appendages intact, but with lungs severely damaged from an antispasm medication he had been prescribed.

My dreams weren't so bad this time. Ralph's legs were still wrapped around my body, but they weren't killing me. Now they were making me short of breath.

✂️∽

Despite our vigilant care, boils appeared on Ralph's groin. I called the home nurse. It took her a few days to get out to the house. By the time she came, the boils had spread between Ralph's legs and below his belly button.

"My, my," she said, peering through her bifocals at Ralph's crotch, "we'll have to keep an eye on these."

Two weeks later, the boils encompassed the lower half of Ralph's body. I called the hospital and made an appointment for surgery. I tried to remain calm, but I was afraid an explosion would occur at any moment. Ralph's boils were about to blow.

Jerry drove Ralph to the hospital. The doctor lanced one boil and said he wanted to see what would happen before he did the others. We booked an appointment for the following week, but the hospital called and canceled. We tried to make another appointment for the next day, but the doctor was busy.

I called a different doctor and raved at him. He got us an appointment that same day. We took Ralph to the hospital, pulled him out of his wheelchair, laid him on a gurney, and undressed him. The doctor called in another doctor. After a long discussion, they lanced all the boils. The room filled with an odor that could have killed a small child. It looked like everything inside Ralph was oozing out.

While the doctors instructed me on how to take care of Ralph's new wounds, Jerry stealthily opened cabinet drawers and closets and swiped bandages, swabs, and tubes of antifungal medicine. When no one but Ralph was looking, he placed the loot in the backpack that hung behind Ralph's wheelchair. Ralph had become Jerry's partner in crime. He enjoyed it. No one at the HMO would have the nerve to accuse Ralph of stealing. He was getting revenge for all the long hours of waiting.

❧

Then bedsores appeared on Ralph's butt. Scarier than the boils, these started from inside the skin and worked their way out. By the time you knew the patient had them, they were full-blown, dangerous, gangrenous blisters. We knew that a bedsore left unattended could cause fever, cold sweats, amputation, and eventually death. Bedsores were a warning that the patient needed to get off the pressure spot immediately.

We snapped into action. We set up appointments with surgeons and skin specialists, and treated his left buttock as if it were a separate entity. We learned the sores were caused by the long hours Ralph spent upright in his wheelchair. So Ralph went to bed earlier and got up later. We planned our weekend schedule around his bedsores and said no to anything that started before 4 P.M. or ended after 10 P.M. Ralph was vigilant. The last thing he wanted to be was completely bedridden.

Laid out flat in his hospital bed, he watched a multitude of movies on the VCR.

But things got worse. One morning, I went downstairs to find Ralph's shoulders covered with ants. I pulled back the sheet and found a full platoon of little black insects crawling up the catheter and swarming over his penis. I quickly smashed as many of them as possible and sprayed the bed bars with Raid.

I went to the store and bought two dozen ant traps. I set them out around the house and hoped that Ralph wouldn't run over them with the wheels of his chair.

Ralph never noticed when the ants were on him. He went about his daily routine of reading the newspaper, watching movies, and sending e-mails. They say ignorance is bliss, and what you don't know can't hurt you. I knew about the ants and it didn't just hurt, it ached.

Ralph's temperature spiked to 104 degrees. He was talking nonsense and didn't seem to hear me when I shouted at him. The sheets underneath him were soaked, his head was on fire, and his body was going into uncontrollable spasms.

I was scared. I called the hospital, and they said they would send the paramedics over as soon as possible. The voice on the other end of the line said I had to get the fever down quickly. "Get some ice and cold towels and put them on his body," the nurse instructed.

Jerry walked into the kitchen as I was staring into the freezer, realizing that we had no ice cubes. "It's show time!" he shouted, grabbing packages of frozen peas and spinach, a loaf of frozen Wonder bread, and an entire frigid salmon—head, tail, and fins. He placed the bag of peas on Ralph's forehead and the salmon across his groin, shoved the solid Wonder bread in his left armpit and the box of spinach in his right. Then he covered Ralph with a thin sheet.

By the time the paramedics arrived, Ralph's temperature had gone down significantly. They slid Ralph onto a gurney and put him in the back of the ambulance. Jerry crawled into the ambulance with Ralph and said he would see me at the hospital.

I put the peas, the spinach, the mushy Wonder bread, and the limp salmon back into the freezer. Then I drove the van to the hospital.

Weeks later, after Ralph was back home, I discovered that Mrs. Scott had used the spinach and peas for stew and Jerry had eaten the Wonder bread. The fish was still in the freezer. I threw it away before Harka could get his hands on it.

Chapter 38

HAPPY BIRTHDAY

Ralph and Harka headed up Telegraph Avenue together. It was Ralph's fifty-fifth birthday, and he was celebrating by taking himself to bookstores, cafés, and yogurt shops near the University of California at Berkeley. But somewhere between Alcatraz and Ashby avenues, Ralph put his wheelchair into high gear with the tilt of his chin and got far ahead of Harka. Harka raced to keep up, only to see Ralph go over a curb, tip sideways, and smash his head against the pavement. He remained strapped inside the wheelchair, unconscious, with blood oozing from his left temple.

Harka ran to Ralph's side and stopped a passing motorist. The motorist called 911, and a policeman arrived almost immediately. He directed traffic around Ralph until an ambulance came. The EMTs righted the wheelchair, lifted Ralph into the vehicle, and rushed off to the hospital.

No one remembered exactly when Ralph came to, but at some point he wailed and cried and shouted that he did not want to be in the hospital. Everyone ignored him.

Harka called me at the gym, and the nightmare of April 27, 1994, started all over again. I jumped into my car and squeezed through the commute traffic over the Bay Bridge. An hour later,

I arrived at the ER just as they were putting the last stitches into Ralph's forehead.

"I want to go home," mumbled Ralph.

"You can't," I answered. "Seven hours haven't gone by, and you know we always spend seven hours in the emergency ward. You'll just have to wait."

My prophecy was right. The paramedics had taken Ralph to the closest hospital, which was not in our HMO. But the routine was familiar; this place worked just like Kaiser. A nurse came into the room and told us the X ray person would be there in thirty minutes. An hour and a half later, the X ray person arrived. A doctor said the IV would be out in fifteen minutes, but forty-five minutes later, long empty, it was still stuck in Ralph's arm. Enormous periods of time elapsed during which no one spoke to us and we had no idea what was going on.

At 10 P.M., a doctor with a clipboard came by. "Mr. Hager, Kaiser wants you in their hospital. You may have to spend the night there. An ambulance will arrive shortly to transport you."

"I don't wanna go. I won't go. I wanna go home." Ralph sounded like a child.

"I'm sorry, Mr. Hager." The doctor spoke in a slow, deliberate tone. "You have a concussion, your core temperature is ninety-three degrees, your urine samples indicate that you might be septic. We can't release you."

"I'm always septic, I'm always cold. I won't go." It was a desperate, Neanderthal wail.

The doctor nodded at me to indicate that we should go outside the room and talk.

In the hallway, he turned to me and said, "If I release him, you must sign papers saying that he was released against our advice and that neither hospital will be liable for further complications. You will have to keep watch over him and not let him fall asleep. You must clean these wounds and call us in three days to find out the results of other tests. Here is a prescription for ciprofloxacin. Kaiser will probably not pay our hospital bill because you refused to go to them. Are you willing to do all this?"

"Yes," I said. "Show me where to sign."

It took another hour to get the papers in order, and an additional hour before two enormous men in weight belts lifted Ralph out of the bed and into the wheelchair.

I rolled Ralph out to the lobby. There was still blood in his ears and his hair. His hospital gown was soaked in urine and his bare bottom showed through the cracks between the armrests and the seat of the wheelchair. With blankets I'd taken from the room where we'd been waiting, I covered him up as best I could.

Ralph shivered and then went to sleep. Ignoring the doctor's orders, I let him rest, while Harka and I waited for Jerry. It would be another hour before he heard our messages on the answering machine and came to our rescue.

I looked at my watch. Exactly seven hours had passed since Ralph had entered the Emergency Room. I leaned over and whispered in his ear, "Happy Birthday, honey."

He grunted, but his eyes remained closed.

Chapter 39

INTERDEPENDENT LIFE

AFTER THE ACCIDENT, MY goal was to help Ralph become as independent as possible and to reinvent our social life. We experimented by going out to dinner, to the movies, and to the theater. But it was hard. Things came to a head one night when we went with friends to a restaurant in San Francisco.

I held the menu up in front of Ralph so that he could read it. A waitress came to our table and asked me if we wanted to order. "No," I answered, "give us another minute."

She came back again to see if we had made up our minds. "Not yet," I said firmly.

She returned a third time. As I gave her the order for Ralph and me, Ralph started to scream. "Son of a bitch, I want to order for myself! Nobody sees me! Nobody pays attention to me! Nobody looks at me! I'm nobody, nobody, nobody!"

He started to cry: big noisy sobs; gulps of air; spitting and snorting and snot running from his nose. The waitress backed off. The manager came around the corner. Our companions and I looked at the floor. There was nothing anyone could do. Ralph had made his point.

After that, I let him order when we went out. Each time a waiter or waitress came to the table, I made sure he or she asked Ralph what we wanted. I let him decide what movies we would see and when we would see them, which television shows we would watch, what we would have for dinner. It seemed fair. He needed some control over his life, and it was the only thing I could give him.

～o～

I gave Ralph almost complete control over our finances. I handed over my paychecks and let him tell me what I owed for expenses. I paid the help.

I thought about hiding money somewhere, but there was so little of it, there was nothing to hide. My parents sent checks, and I spent them immediately on toilet paper and Kleenex, ant spray and coffee. My mother and I discussed setting up an investment fund for me, but the truth was I needed the cash now.

In the beginning, when Ralph's health was more precarious and I was only working part-time, I would come home to a litany of complaints. Ralph would launch into all that was wrong with his life: Harka was too slow getting him up in the mornings and Jerry was forgetful; Mrs. Scott got on his nerves and I wasn't home enough; no one helped him open his mail or kept his desk orderly; his computer wasn't working right, the intercom was scratchy, the TV remote was out of reach, and he was never comfortable in his chair.

Talking about the problems was almost as depressing as living with them. A therapist suggested we time our discussions. Ralph would get fifteen minutes, and then I would have fifteen minutes. But a quarter of an hour was too long, and by the time Ralph was through, I was too exhausted, angry, and tired to respond.

When we started hooking lights, TVs, VCRs, and telephones

to Ralph's computer, things began to change. Now when I came home, Ralph was watching a video. I was not to talk with him until it was over. I went to the kitchen and made dinner, set the table, carried the plates to the dining room. When the video was over, we put in another or turned on the news. During commercials, I would hear about Ralph's day, then I'd go back into the kitchen, put away the leftovers and clean up the mess. I gave him his pills and stretched his arms, put in another video for him, said I was tired, and went to bed.

The monotony of our evenings was slowly killing me.

~oo~

To say our social life changed would be an understatement. A single invitation to a party from two old friends required research on our options before we could accept.

We had been told there would be a few steps we would have to climb to get inside. But when we arrived at the party, across the bay in Marin County, we found eighteen steep, narrow brick stairs to the front yard and another four wooden ones to the front door.

I was furious. How could anyone be so stupid to think that Ralph and I could negotiate this stairway? We'd been promised half a dozen strong, healthy males to carry Ralph and his wheelchair up the path, but I could tell they weren't going to have an easy time of it.

Our helpers gathered around Ralph and discussed how they would maneuver him up the steps. As we sat outside in the cold, it became clear that no one was sure we would succeed. Finally, in one gargantuan effort, Ralph was heaved up the staircase and onto the lawn. His carriers sat and rested before negotiating the final four steps.

I ran back and forth from the van to the house, carrying

supplies. The living room was crammed with furniture. Guests moved chairs, couches, and end tables against the walls. When Ralph entered the redecorated room, he became its centerpiece, surrounded by well-wishers. I sneaked into the kitchen and gulped down two strong margaritas.

I returned to the living room and took my place behind Ralph on the couch. I stayed there as the party progressed, and drank as many margaritas as were handed to me. Someone turned up the CD-player and couples started to sway to the music.

After a while, the crowd felt claustrophobic. Before everyone became inebriated, we asked for help in getting out of the house. We chose the least-intoxicated party guests, and stumbled with them out to the front porch.

Ralph made it over the first four steps with not much problem, but again, our volunteers needed to discuss how they would carry Ralph down the eighteen remaining steps. Finally, a plan was made, the stairway carefully negotiated, and Ralph and the wheelchair set down on the sidewalk.

Winded, the helpers congratulated one another for a job well done. A few of them walked us to the van and watched as I put down the lift, rolled Ralph onto it, raised him, wheeled him in, and strapped him down.

I wasn't sober, but no one seemed to notice. I backed the van out of the driveway, onto the tree-lined street, waved goodbye to everyone and gunned the engine. Somehow, I drove over the Richmond–San Rafael Bridge, negotiated the highway lanes onto highway 24, then off on Martin Luther King, left onto 54th Street, right onto Dover, and to our driveway.

I got out of the van, pulled down the lift, backed Ralph out, and brought him down. I opened the screen door for him, took off his glasses and his hat, gave him his mouth stick, and turned on the television set. Then I went back out to the van to turn off the engine and gather up all of Ralph's survival gear. It was only then that I noticed that I had driven all the way home without the headlights on.

Knowing how drunk I was, I wondered how my friends had allowed Ralph and me to get in the van and drive home. But I had a feeling they were glad to get rid of us. No one likes to dance while a person in a wheelchair is watching.

∽◦∾

Ralph and I went to a lot of weddings, because weddings are almost always wheelchair-accessible. They gave us a chance to get out and see people.

But wedding ceremonies became very painful for me because I never had a dance partner and because I listened too hard to what the bride and groom promised one another. When they repeated "in sickness and in health," I wondered if anyone could ever really make such a pledge without knowing the consequences.

I tried to remember if I had actually said "in sickness and in health," and whether it mattered now. Our wedding had been a casual affair at the courthouse, attended by bride, groom, and a dragged-in witness. I couldn't remember if, in civil ceremonies, one promised things, like "for better for worse, in sickness and in health, until death do us part."

Long ago, it had been simple for me to leave my first husband over things that now seemed insignificant: different goals, too little money, not enough fun. How was it that I was able to leave him so easily and yet couldn't leave Ralph? I had so many reasons to go.

But I stay. For how long, I don't know.

Chapter 40

CHRISTOPHER REEVE

A YEAR AFTER RALPH's bicycle wreck, Christopher Reeve had a horseback-riding accident. The news said that people from all over the world were sending Christopher Reeve get-well cards and money.

I bought *People* magazine. Christopher Reeve and his beautiful wife were featured on the cover. I drank two Bloody Marys and read about how their house was being remodeled to make it wheelchair-accessible.

Barbara Walters interviewed Reeve and his family. Film clips showed images of the renovated house and all the neat equipment he had to keep himself alive. He was working with the world's leading authorities on spinal-cord injuries. They were hopeful.

Mrs. Reeve said that sex was still possible and she planned to have another baby.

For the Academy Awards ceremony, Christopher Reeve and his wife were flown out to Hollywood in a private Lear jet. He was dressed in a black tuxedo, with satin stripes down the legs of his pants. He gave a moving speech to the audience. An enthusiastic commentator mentioned that Mr. Reeve was directing a film and doing the voice-over of a cartoon character for a soon-to-be-released Hollywood blockbuster.

But underneath the formal black tuxedo, I knew there were tubes running from Christopher Reeve's penis to a bag taped to his unmoving leg, just like Ralph's. And I also knew that several people had worked like hell to twist his limbs into the black suit. And an army of folks had made millions of arrangements and jumped through multiple hoops to wrestle Christopher Reeve into that private Lear jet, fly him out to Hollywood, and roll him onto the empty stage.

And the elegant Mrs. Reeve, who was described by the press as radiant and charming, and oh-so-incredibly responsible for her husband's care, was probably dying inside, just like me.

Chapter 41

Quad Life

Wʜᴀᴛ ꜱᴇᴛ Rᴀʟᴘʜ ᴀᴘᴀʀᴛ as a quad was his affability, we were told. This surprised me, because before his accident, he had been demanding and impatient with people. But Ralph was smart and rarely let emotions get in the way of accomplishing his plans, even when his daily mission was limited to getting out of bed by 1 ᴘ.ᴍ. If meeting his goals meant being as easy as possible with people, he was more than willing to go the distance.

Most quadriplegics have some use of their fingers or hands, since those with more severe injuries—such as Ralph and Christopher Reeve—tend to die. Those with a smidgen of movement are easier to work for. They can help with bed and wheelchair transfers. They can lift spoons and forks and sometimes glasses. They can scribble notes with special pens and notepads. Some can even drive, using specially equipped vans that cost more money than most of us could afford.

Mickey Donnetello could lift a coffee cup to his lips and pick up his bum legs and place one across the other, making him look comfortable in his wheelchair.

Drew could write with a pen and use a regular computer. Harvey could light a Camel unfiltered cigarette and smoke, which he did, one after another. I suspected that our former acquaintance, Stuart, could use a hypodermic needle, but I wasn't sure.

We heard of a quad who sold drugs for a living to Berkeley High School students and one who was finishing up a Master of Fine Arts degree at U.C. Berkeley. He held the brush in his mouth and painted on a huge canvas propped against a wall.

Jerry told us about Angus, a quadriplegic he had worked for, who demanded that Jerry button his shirts from the bottom up. If Jerry started to button the shirt from the neck down, Angus would scream at him to stop and force him to restart at the bottom.

When putting on a sweater, Angus wanted his left arm placed in the sleeve first. If Jerry started on the right, again Angus would remind him of his mistake. Angus's right shoe had to be put on first and taken off last. Rules with no purpose other than control kept Angus and his mother from holding on to any help for longer than a few days.

Rick lived in an upscale neighborhood in Berkeley, in a small cottage his parents had built for him behind their own sprawling mansion. It was a beautiful place, containing all the latest electronic gear. Rick could control his environment with a computer attached to his wheelchair. Before his accident, he had aspirations, as well as the talent and good looks, to become a politician. After his accident, he created architechtural renderings on a specially designed keyboard.

He had a custom-made bathroom with a wheelchair-accessible shower in which he liked to bathe at least twice a day, a normal activity for the able-bodied but an undertaking that required eight wheelchair transfers for his help. His parents paid well, but most attendants shied away from so much lifting. Jerry had stopped working for Rick because he didn't like the neighborhood. "Nothin' was happenin' there," he said.

There were quads who didn't pay what they had promised, and quads who were so depressed they made the people around them miserable. Some quads lived in squalor. Others lived with relatives who scared potential attendants away. Many quads were overweight, making them difficult to move. Some quads were so needy for friendship and companionship they frightened the help. The more stories I heard, the more I understood how lucky we were. Ralph's good humor, lack of demands, and willingness to compromise were keeping us afloat.

∽o∾

On the weekends, my single friends scoured the personal ads for the perfect match; my rich friends checked the restaurant reviews to decide where they would next dine; my curious friends read the sex advice column; Ralph studied the movie reviews; I always turned to the Attendants Wanted column.

The *Express* weekly allowed disabled people to place ads free of charge. After Ralph's accident, we had taken advantage of this service. Thanks to Jerry and Harka, we hadn't had to use it in a long time.

I recognized the names that appeared every week. We knew many of the disabled; others were famous by reputation. Some advertised without stating their names, but we were aware of their stories, too. They were the ones who had so much trouble keeping attendants, they didn't want anyone to know they were looking again. Caregivers and potential attendants shared stories about the demands and cheapness of certain disabled residents. If you had a bad reputation, you didn't want to place your name in the ad.

Hiring and keeping help is one of the most difficult and painful tasks of the disabled and their loved ones. How can you trust a person you don't know with the most intimate, important needs of your existence? We heard stories about abusive attendants, insane help, and no-good employees. We had first-hand experience with alcoholics, drug addicts, thieves, liars, the mentally ill, and con artists. As we got more acquainted with the disabled community, we shared references and horror stories.

Drew told us how he always interviewed attendants at cafés, because one applicant had curled up in Drew's fireplace and he had to call the police to have the man removed.

Wages for attendants varied, from seven dollars an hour for those who were subsidized by the government, to twelve dollars for those who had huge out-of-court settlements or insurance plans that covered home care. We were right in the middle. Attendants weren't covered on our health plan, and we hadn't sued anybody, because the accident hadn't been anyone's fault. But we had steady income from Ralph's pension and from my job.

When we ran into Drew at the movies one day, the subject quickly turned to attendants, as it usually did.

Drew asked us how we were doing with help. "Very well," answered Ralph, "how about you?"

"Well, I'm looking for someone in the mornings now. I finally got the weekend evening shift filled, but as soon as I get one slot taken care of, I have another opening."

"We've been very lucky," Ralph said. "Jerry has been with us for over two years, and Harka has been around for almost a year. They cover everything."

"You're kidding!" said Drew incredulously. "What do you pay them?"

"About eight-fifty an hour, but we loan them money constantly, pay for parking tickets and child-support payments, allow them to use our van, buy their favorite foods, and try to keep them as happy as possible. If we run out of something they like, Suzy goes to the store and buys it for them before she leaves for work."

"Sounds to me like you people need to set some boundaries," said Drew solemnly. "Your attendants are running your lives."

I looked at Drew. "There aren't any boundaries at our house," I said slowly. "And if I had a million dollars and Jerry asked me for it with the promise he'd take care of Ralph for the rest of his life, I'd give it to him."

"Well, I'd be careful if I were you," said Drew. "You haven't been at this game as long as me. But I have to go now. If I don't get home soon, my attendant will leave before he's put me to bed, and I'll be calling you for some help."

Chapter 42

ACTIVISM

Rᴀʟᴘʜ ᴀɴᴅ ʜɪs ᴡʜᴇᴇʟᴄʜᴀɪʀ were always getting stuck in tight spots. He'd been stranded in elevators at the Downtown Berkeley BART station and at the Landmark Theater on Center Street. He'd been caught in the revolving doors at Nordstrom's, trapped in a cattle guard on the Nimitz Trail, and lost on the third floor of the student union building at U.C. Berkeley until someone heard his screams and came to save him. He was constantly snared in the street drains found at the base of many curb cuts.

So when he said he wanted to help change things, to be an activist for the disabled community, I went along with it. I was proud of him.

We arranged to go to an A's game. We'd heard the Coliseum had put in an $850,000 outdoor elevator that didn't always work. The team's owners had set aside a desirable block of seats, but they made it nearly impossible for the disabled to purchase them. You had to pick the tickets up in person rather than over the telephone like able-bodied people. It wasn't fair.

I started to resent what Ralph's activism meant to me. Now I had to yell at the box-office lady when she told me certain seats weren't available to people in wheelchairs and then go down to the Coliseum to buy the tickets in person. The day of the game, I had to rush home from work early; put Ralph in the van; gather up blankets, shawls, sweaters, hats, pills, and water; hide beer in the bottom of his backpack; put guacamole and potato salad in Tupperware containers; find plastic forks and cups.

One mile down the freeway, we slammed into the biggest traffic jam imaginable. I could hear the water running out of our leaky radiator.

Ralph, trapped in the back with no windows to see outside, wanted an update. People in sharp little cars squeezed me in from all sides. The passenger's side mirror was crooked. The rearview mirror had long ago fallen off, and the radio was nothing but a bunch of cut wires.

When we finally got to the Coliseum, the parking lot was full, half the spaces taken by tailgate parties. I couldn't believe what I was seeing. People eating hot dogs in an asphalt wasteland.

Of course, there were no disabled spaces left. The city had given out more placards than there were spots in the entire county. I found a space so far away we could just barely make out the Coliseum on the horizon. I unstrapped Ralph and carried two bags of food and clothing across the acres of boiling hot pavement. There were more concrete barriers in the parking lot than there are land mines in a Cambodian rice paddy.

Finally, we arrived at the outdoor elevator. We found someone to operate it, and *bam*, it stopped dead in its tracks only a few feet up. Ralph was suspended in the air, above the crowds. He didn't have such a bad view, but we wondered how he was ever going to get down.

The operator radioed security. Security radioed a mechanic. The A's scored a phenomenal fifteen runs in the second inning and Ralph saw half of it from his perch above the masses. Ten guys surrounded us, working on the lift.

But I wasn't upset because I didn't have to do anything except watch the game. It was relaxing. No bags to carry, no pills to give. Ralph was too high to reach. There were no questions to answer, and all those nice men were helping us. Once in a while I yelled at someone just to look like I was busy. But basically I'd found inner peace in the Barbecue Patio section of the Coliseum, with Ralph suspended above me.

Out of the corner of my eye, I could see people in the stands staring at Ralph, hoping that poor pathetic man in the wheelchair didn't fall onto their heads.

I knew what they were thinking.

They were thinking, if it were me, I'd shoot myself. But they didn't know that was impossible. Shooting Ralph was my responsibility, because Ralph couldn't lift a gun to his head. I'd have to do it.

I watched Mark McGwire hit a line drive to third base and move his strapping body to first. I looked up at my helpless, patient husband, frozen above the crowd. I realized that if there was going to be any activism in our lives, it had to begin with me. I needed to learn to say no.

∽∘∾

In 1996, Ralph was appointed to the board of directors at the Center for Independent Living in Berkeley. I volunteered to help. I thought it was something we could do together.

I was assigned to the fundraising committee. At my first meeting, we discussed plans for CIL's twenty-fifth anniversary. We talked about marching down Telegraph Avenue, throwing a big party, and inviting disabled celebrities. Someone mentioned Christopher Reeve. Everyone laughed except me. I didn't get the joke.

"What's so funny?" I asked. "Someone needs to fill me in on the politics of this. I'm new to the disabled community and I don't know the skinny on everything."

"Well," said a man who used a cane, "Christopher Reeve thinks he'll walk again. We need to write him a letter and set him straight."

"Oh yeah," murmured everyone in unison.

"Set him straight about what?" I asked.

"That he isn't going to walk again. That he's disabled just like the rest of us. He needs to know that all his money and fame don't make him any better." Heads that could nodded in agreement.

I thought about his comment for a moment. "Wait," I said. "Isn't that just hope? Isn't he hopeful that he'll walk again? The accident was only a year ago. Ralph thought he would walk again, too."

As I said these words, I realized that Ralph and I had lost hope. Or maybe we had just accepted reality. I was getting confused. I admired Christopher Reeve and his wife for their optimism and their ability to reach out and tell their story. But I was jealous that they got so much attention from the experts and that money seemed not to be a problem. Christopher Reeve probably had a retrofitted bathroom in which he could actually take a bath. I knew that if Christopher Reeve ever did walk again, I'd suspect that his money and fame had gotten him better care than Ralph and I could get.

And then I said something that I immediately regretted. "Well, when you write that letter, let me know," I said sarcastically, "because I want to include a letter to Mrs. Reeve. I want to find out how she has such great sex."

Everybody laughed. I had made a joke at Christopher Reeve's

expense. I had made fun of a man who was more helpless than my husband. Christopher Reeve couldn't even breathe on his own.

I was starting to fit in with the disabled community. I didn't like what I was becoming.

Chapter 43

NAVIGATING

We HEADED TO AN art film at the Embarcadero Center Cinema in San Francisco. Nothing would happen in the film. French people would smoke cigarettes, eat good food, consume dark bottles of cabernet, and act blasé. I'd be bored, resentful, tired, and sad. Ralph would fall asleep and I would have a headache and once again nothing would get done around our home.

At the building complex that housed the movie theater, the elevator was broken. Through the nearby intercom, we called security. They promised to have it fixed in thirty minutes; forty minutes later, through the crackling speaker, they told us it was impossible. The elevator was on seismic mode and wasn't going anywhere.

Twenty-two escalator steps separated us from the movie theater. I shouted into the wall. "Isn't there an alternative route up to the theater that you can help us with?"

"Sorry, ma'am. There's no way."

"Well, how can that be? This isn't an old building. Surely, there must be some way up. How does a disabled person get down if they are up on the second floor and the elevator doesn't work?"

"We call the paramedics."

"Well, then, call them now."

But I didn't mean it, and they knew it. Because, after all, this wasn't an emergency situation. It was just a man in a wheelchair who couldn't get where he wanted to go.

I asked if there were working elevators in Embarcadero Two, an adjacent building linked to One by a walkway. "And if so," I said to the voice inside the wall, "can't we walk over from One to Two? And aren't there a few steps in between? Surely you'll help us with those?"

A new voice came through the speaker. The voice introduced himself as Head of Security. "No," said the voice.

"No?" I asked. "Why the hell not?"

"Liability," it said.

"What's the difference between liability and helping a fellow human being get where he wants to go?" I asked.

"Lawyers," said Head of Security.

But I did get Ralph to the movie. We went over to Embarcadero Two and entered the service elevator. We got off on the mezzanine and headed toward Embarcadero One. When we arrived at the six steps that separated Embarcadero One from Embarcadero Two, I went into a nearby Mexican restaurant and convinced five young men to leave their margaritas and help us. Together they heaved Ralph over the first set of steps, rested, and then carried him down the last six. I thanked them.

Ralph motored over to the ticket counter. We were escorted to the back of the building, through a service entrance, and down a long dark hallway to the theater. Ralph's wheelchair didn't fit inside the house elevator.

Ralph was delighted to be at the movies. But I wasn't so

happy. I kept wondering about how we would get home once the picture ended.

∽o∾

Another night, Ralph and I went to a movie at a different San Francisco theater, Opera Plaza. Upon arrival, we learned the show was sold out. I approached the front counter and asked if any wheelchair seats might still be available. "Probably," replied the ticket seller. "Let me call my supervisor."

The manager came out the front door and looked at Ralph and me. "I'm sorry," she said. "There are no seats left. We are sold out."

"Not even a place for a wheelchair?" I asked. "Are you sure there aren't nondisabled people in the disabled seats?"

"It doesn't matter," she explained as if she were talking to a three-year-old child. "After a certain point, we sell all the seats to whoever is here. You should have arrived earlier."

"Wait," I said, "no offense, but I think that's illegal. I was here plenty early, but there isn't a single disabled parking spot within miles of this place. But that's beside the point. I don't think you can sell those seats to nondisabled people."

"Please don't get defensive," the manager said defensively. "Perhaps I don't know the law. But I will certainly find out tomorrow."

"Tomorrow isn't good enough," I pronounced firmly.

The entire conversation went on over Ralph's head. He couldn't hear what was discussed so he sat passively while I defended his rights. The line of people waiting for the next show stared at us. A nice-looking couple at the ticket window listened intensely, and when they saw we weren't leaving, they approached us. "Pardon me," said the handsome man. "I couldn't help overhearing what was going on. I believe we bought the last tickets to the show. Please take ours and we'll come back for the second screening."

"Thank you," answered the manager quickly, before I had time to reply. She turned to me and said "Come on in." She opened the exit door for us to enter.

"I don't know," I hesitated, "this isn't right." But before I could protest more, the magnanimous couple disappeared. I could just barely glimpse their well-dressed backs as they walked hand-in-hand away from us.

"Let's go," said Ralph. He almost knocked me over heading into the lobby.

Once Ralph had backed into the wheelchair space and I had adjusted his wraps and settled into the seat beside him, I looked around the small dark theater. I could see two empty spaces for wheelchairs, plus an unoccupied seat.

After the film ended, and we waited, as always, for the entire theater to clear before we made our departure, I said to Ralph, "I'm going to find the manager and tell her there were seats available throughout the film and there was always a space for you and your wheelchair, even before those nice people gave us their tickets."

"Yeah, do that," said Ralph.

We went out to the lobby and asked an usher to find the manager. While we waited, a woman who had watched our confrontation before the start of the movie greeted us. "You were right," she said, smiling. "That was illegal. She can't sell those seats to nondisabled people. Those seats belong to you. And then to force you to accept charity—how humiliating. You don't want charity. You want what is rightfully yours."

I held my tongue. I wanted to tell her that I didn't mind accepting charity once in a while. In fact, I wouldn't mind accepting a lot of charity: a few free movie tickets; someone else to drive the van and fight for a parking spot; enough money to redo the bathroom, buy an electric door, pay off the credit-card bills; a new house with wider door frames and no steps; a van that was reliable and had a radio; extra cash to buy a plane ticket and leave Ralph at home with Harka and Jerry. Just what I needed. No, I didn't mind accepting the tickets from that nice young couple. I imagined that we had made them feel good about themselves. A little generosity can work both ways.

❦

After a trip to the movies another night, Ralph got stuck on the van lift in our driveway. I was already angry about everything. I was mad that I had to get down on my hands and knees and unstrap the wheelchair, pissed off that it was 11 P.M. and I still had to make dinner and feed him, furious that I didn't have a life, didn't have any money, and didn't have much in the way of friends.

Ralph had gone forward on the lift when he should have gone backward. The front wheels of his chair fell into a space between the bumper and the lift. He was wedged in tight. There was no way I could move him.

"Goddamn it!" I shouted into his face, standing on the edge of the bumper, leaning forward from inside the van. "I'll never get you out! Goddamn it!"

"Sorry," said Ralph softly. "I didn't mean to do it. I was trying to help you, Suzy. Don't get upset. We'll think of something."

"Like what?" I hissed. "Jerry and Harka aren't home. We're all alone. It's too late to get a neighbor. I'll have to call 911."

Before Ralph could answer, I stomped up the ramp, into the

house and called the emergency number. I listened to a recording. How ironic. I always got an answering service when I called 911. What was the point?

Finally, a live voice responded. "My husband is stuck on the lift of our van," I explained. "He's quadriplegic. He can't move. I can't get him off. We need help." I surprised myself by the matter-of-factness of my speech.

"All right," said the person on the other end. "What's your address? I'll have someone over as soon as possible."

I returned to the van. Ralph waited silently above me, stoic as always. He looked forward into the van, frozen in his wheelchair. I paced up and down the driveway. I should put a shawl around Ralph's shoulders, I thought, but I didn't.

The police arrived much sooner than I expected. Two bulky men in thick blue uniforms climbed out of the squad car. They ambled up the driveway. "What seems to be the problem, ma'am?" asked the taller officer.

"My husband is stuck on the lift," I said, peering through the darkness toward them. "I can't move him by myself. Sorry about this, but we're desperate."

"No problem." The shorter policeman looked up at Ralph. "Can you hear me, sir? We'll get you down in a minute."

"Oh, yes," replied Ralph in a strong voice. "I can hear you. I'm okay. My wife is a little upset, but I'm fine."

The smaller officer stood by the lift while his partner crawled into the van's side door.

"Here you go, sir," said the officer. He lifted the front of the wheelchair and shoved it back. "All set?"

"Yes, indeed," answered Ralph buoyantly.

I pushed the lift button and Ralph came down.

"Thank you," I said to the policemen. "Sorry to bother you."

"Yeah, thanks," added Ralph. He put his chair in gear and started up the ramp to our back door.

"No problem. Anytime. You folks take care now." Both policemen nodded politely.

I closed the van doors and watched the officers walk down our driveway. It was quiet on our block. A full moon filled the night sky above the house across the street. My garden smelled damp and sweet.

Ralph waited for me at the door. I unlocked it and let us in, then bolted it shut behind us. One day at a time, I said to myself. One day at a time. To Ralph I said, "I'm sorry I got upset. That wasn't fair. Sometimes I just flip out."

"It's okay, sweetheart," he answered, his voice firm and decisive. "Turn on the TV. Get me my mouth stick. Put the key back in the wheelchair pocket. Take off this hat. What shall we have for dinner?"

I felt the anger well up inside me again. It tasted bitter and harsh. I pushed it back down and went into the kitchen to make dinner.

∽༠∾

A few weeks later, I left Ralph in a parking lot, listening to a homeless man, while I searched for the elevator up to the trendy restaurant we were going to.

We had learned that homeless people felt a kinship with us. When Ralph rolled by someone begging, they stopped asking for spare change and whispered, "God bless you." We were with them, down and out, at the bottom of the food chain.

It didn't matter how much money we had. Even the destitute felt good around Ralph. While other people jogged over us and hurried past with eyes looking anywhere but at us, the outcasts and the downtrodden stared into our faces and said, "Good day, brother and sister, good day."

So it was with the toothless man in the parking lot. I could hear him chattering away with Ralph, telling him how fortunate he was and how the good-Lord-willing would provide, and on and on and on.

I took my time.

When I returned, the derelict was repeating himself. Ralph looked trapped, as always.

"Get me out of here," he hissed as I put myself between him and the man.

I got behind the wheelchair and gave it a push. The ragged fellow continued to talk.

"There goes a lucky man," he said.

"Hardly," I answered, looking back over my shoulder. I had put some distance between us and this poor soul.

But he shouted across the parking lot, "Oh yeah, he be a lucky man, he be a blessed man. And you know how I know?"

We didn't answer. We were almost out of earshot.

"I know'd he be a lucky man," he cried out after us. "He be lucky 'cause he got you."

Chapter 44

THE BIRD

RALPH DOESN'T REMEMBER THIS, but it was actually my idea that he get a bird. I didn't think he'd take me up on it. But I should have known better. I should have known right away what kind of bird Ralph would want.

Everyone had suggested we get a dog. We had tried to do so almost as soon as we returned home from the hospital. I completed all the papers for a Canine Companion while Ralph was in a drug-induced haze. I got three letters of recommendation, sent in a check for forty-five dollars, and wrote an essay on why we wanted and needed a dog.

We'd heard there was a two-year wait, so we wanted to start early. We rushed to Santa Rosa for the interview and tour. But, it turns out, Canine Companions aren't for everyone. We weren't told this before we arrived, completed the application, sent in the check for forty-five dollars, got the three letters of recommendation, and wrote the essay on how and why we needed a dog: Ralph was "too disabled" to have a Canine Companion.

But, I rationalized, we didn't really want a dog anyway. What we wanted was a bird.

Ralph took up his search for the perfect bird as he did everything else. With my support, he joined bird groups on the

Internet and chatted with people who owned birds. I took him to bookstores, libraries, and pet shops.

My brother, the budding veterinarian, warned me that "bird people were weird" and that I should watch where and how I stepped. He was right. "Bird people" gave me the willies, and all birds, except lovebirds, made me nervous.

But Ralph liked them and wanted to become a bird person himself. That's why we found ourselves one sunny afternoon in an exotic pet store on Fillmore Street in San Francisco, staring into the eyes not of a cockatiel, but of a tall, long-haired man named Randy. He was thin. His nose was sharp and beakish.

Randy showed Ralph every bird in the store, starting with tiny blue parakeets and gradually moving toward bigger, more monstrous and vicious African parrots, Asian cockatoos, and South American macaws. Randy said he needed to get to know a potential bird owner before he sold that person a bird. It was essential that he familiarize himself with Ralph's habits and values. He needed to "contemplate Ralph's essence and gaze into his soul."

Randy peered into Ralph's pale face with his beady gray eyes and saw the proud owner of the biggest, most expensive bird in the store, a royal blue macaw. It was only two grand, in a cage as big as our dining room.

"Ralph," I whispered into his ear as he studied the electric-striped gold and azure macaw, "shouldn't we consider something smaller and less expensive? Shouldn't we find a bird that doesn't require an indoor football field and a small forest to survive? Shouldn't we get a bird that won't stick its talons into your neck or poke your eyeballs out, a bird that doesn't screech when the sun comes up and won't learn to curse like a sailor? What about a bird whose turds are smaller than pears? Ralph, think of me. Who is going to wrestle this bird to the ground after it pecks your cheeks to a bloody pulp, destroys your wheelchair, and makes a mess all over our wall-to-wall carpet? Please, Ralph, let's consider a cat, a mouse, a soft little bunny rabbit."

But it was too late. Randy had moved his skinny body between us and was making his sales pitch.

"Ralph," he said seriously, kneeling down so that his earnest face was directly in front of Ralph's. "When you first came in here, I thought, here's a man who needs a little bird, something to warm him up before he goes for the big enchilada. But after spending this quality time with you, and after getting to know your inner psyche, I can see that you and I are very similar. When I wanted to buy a motorcycle, my friends said, 'Randy, get a Honda, something small you can handle.' But I went out and bought the biggest fucking Harley-Davidson I could get my hands on, and I think you, Ralph, should buy the biggest motherfucking bird you can get, and that's why I think you should buy this macaw."

And that's what Ralph did. He named it Lolita.

∽o∾

Soon, Ralph had to hire Salina, a Brazilian woman, to clean Lolita's bird cage when Jerry and I refused to do it. Harka was afraid of her. In his country you ate birds like Lolita, you didn't keep them as pets. It made sense to hire someone from South America to tidy up after a South American bird, even if it didn't make sense to have a bird that required full-time help.

Salina was wonderful: loud, boisterous, full of life and energy. When she was in the house there was no room for Mrs. Scott. Her first words to Ralph were, "You know, I think we have lots in common, you and me, Ralph, because I am a Trekkie and you are a nuclear physicist. Together we have lots we can *deeeescuss*."

There was lots of chatter and laughter because Salina was a talker, and she talked and talked and talked, to Ralph, to the bird, to Jerry, to me. And while she talked, she cleaned. It was a good thing she was young and energetic, because the bird shit needed to be sandblasted to remove it from the cage.

Salina came to clean the cage two times a week, but we had to hire her for a third day as well. By the end of the weekend, the house reeked so badly of bird shit, we couldn't wait for Salina to show up on Monday. At least we didn't have to worry about the house smelling like Ralph's urine anymore.

But Lolita did not bond with Ralph, Salina, Harka, Mrs. Scott, or me. She fell in love with Jerry. In the morning, she came down off her perch, crawled up his leg and over his belly, and mounted his shoulder. There she stayed as Jerry bathed and oiled Ralph, gave him his medications, strapped him into his wheelchair, prepared and fed him his first meal of the day.

Lolita ate breakfast at noon with Ralph, then went upstairs and took a nap with Jerry. She cooed and fluttered and licked him with her wicked little tongue. She rubbed her brilliantly golden head against his thick neck.

Lolita was rotten to everyone else. The moment I got near her, she attacked me and clawed at my earrings, my wedding ring, and the buttons on my blouse; she plucked the letters A, F, and G off Ralph's keyboard; she chewed the molding off the wall beside her cage; she tore apart the telephone book and cut important wires on Ralph's wheelchair, which had to be repaired by a specialist. Harka and Mrs. Scott gave her plenty of space. But to Jerry she remained faithful, dependent, and true, like the rest of us.

Chapter 45

OUR KIND OF PLACE

It WAS TWO YEARS after Ralph's accident before we started venturing back into San Francisco on a regular basis. Parking was horrendous and finding disabled spaces a chore. But gradually, I grew bolder and more aggressive. When garage attendants told me I couldn't park in their spaces because the van was too big, I held my ground until they had no choice but to succumb. Sometimes, I simply pretended I did not understand their broken English or sweeping gestures and drove in as though I were entitled to any spot in the place.

I found the locations of the disabled signs in every neighborhood, and made beelines for blue curbs. I discovered where senior citizen centers and government offices were located, and I learned that parking in front of churches was always a good bet. Still, I had to be quick and bold and daring.

We went to Chinatown, the Mission, Fisherman's Wharf, and Ghirardelli Square. Immigrants, tourists, and children stared at us; within the financial district, we were deliberately ignored; in Macy's, we were trampled upon; and at 18th and Castro streets, no one noticed us at all.

Golden Gate Park was too cold and foggy; upper Fillmore

and Pacific Heights were uncomfortably hilly; the theater district was dangerous; and South Park was crowded.

It was in North Beach that we finally found a comfort zone. One foggy afternoon, Ralph and I were struggling over a small incline on the corner of Grant and Columbus streets. We looked up and saw the swinging doors of The Saloon. We peeked inside. It was dark and loud. People moved bar stools, chairs, and tables so that Ralph could squeeze by. We passed leather-clad motorcyclists, neighborhood sex workers, poorly dressed tourists, sailors, and old men in shiny suits, their greasy hair swept into pompadours above bulbous, pocked, purple-veined noses. We settled into a corner, across from the small stage where Bobby Spiro and the Racquet Players pounded out the blues.

I shouted an order to a scantily clad waitress—an Anchor Steam for Ralph, a glass of house red for me. The bass guitarist, with a hairdo like Bozo the Clown, stepped forward off the stage, nodded at Ralph, and plucked his guitar into a high-pitched cry.

All the band members looked gray and puffy. Between songs, some of them drank iced tea and water. Others had pitchers of beer conveniently close to their instruments. The lead singer sipped something stronger. They smiled at us, and stopped by our table during breaks to introduce themselves. We learned that they had been playing the same songs, in the same spot, since 1968.

Everyone in the bar seemed nice, so we decided to go back the next Sunday and the next, until we became regulars, looking forward to weekend afternoons at The Saloon, when Bobby Spiro and the Racquet Players played for tips and free booze. The price was right. There was no cover charge or two-drink minimum. We could sit there all day, watch the crowd change, listen to the music, daydream. No one gave us any trouble.

The waitress service was unreliable, so I often bussed our own table and those around us. When the last set was through and the band packed up and headed for another gig, we went out into the foggy night and found a quiet place to eat and rest our eardrums.

In the Italian restaurants of North Beach, we discovered waiters, waitresses, bartenders, and maitre d's who made us feel welcome. The waitstaff at Mario's Cigar Store practically carried Ralph inside. At Cafe Freddy's, the bartender came outside with a hammer and pried open a side door so that Ralph could enter. Some places served us complimentary wine; a waiter slipped Ralph a special appetizer; another gave him extra biscotti; someone pinned a carnation on his sweater.

Between sets at The Saloon, we got to know the band. Billy Webb played a Yamaha organ and looked like William Burroughs. Freddy Shoemaker beat the drums and explained to us his recent triumph over a twenty-five-year heroin addiction. Bobby Spiro, clad in sneakers and a glow-in-the-dark Earth Day T-shirt, claimed to have once played with Steve Miller, Boz Scaggs, and Jethro Tull. Treefrog, the lead singer, nodded to us as he ambled out the door for a blast of nicotine and weed. Wally Tate, his ruffled shirt soaked with sweat, pulled up a chair and told us about his kids. He introduced us to Billy's girlfriend, Sheila, a woman who looked twice his age, carried a black plastic Harrod's shopping bag, and never took off her extra-thick, prescription sunglasses. She reminisced about trysts with Jack Kerouac and Allen Ginsberg, before Ginsberg announced he was gay and Kerouac drank himself to death.

Sometimes the band members changed: there'd be a trumpet player one week, replaced by two saxophonists the following

Sunday; occasionally an enormous woman with a huge gap between her teeth belted out *"Momma, she treats yo' daughter mean."* Another afternoon, a tiny gal from Texas sang in a voice that shook the dance floor as well as the building next door; a man carrying a beat-up Adidas gym bag and wearing decaying basketball shoes wailed in a desperate, eerie voice incoherent lyrics about loss and love; a young, pale man, nattily dressed in sports jacket, tie, overcoat, and scarf swished in, mounted the stage, and sang plaintively that if it wasn't for bad luck, he'd have no luck at all.

Everyone in the bar danced. Now and then, I jitterbugged with Sheila and sometimes, I danced by myself. Once, I bobbed around the wooden floor with a woman who squirmed and writhed as if she worked at Big Al's, the strip joint down the street. I slow-danced with the man with the Adidas gym bag and partnered with Treefrog when he wasn't singing. Sometimes, Ralph went out on the floor and manipulated his wheelchair back and forth and side to side. Everyone had to move out of his way or risk being knocked over.

The Saloon was now our place. It was full of losers, outcasts, weirdos, and people who didn't quite fit the norm. We basked in the glow of their camaraderie and acceptance. Week after week, we returned, even when there was no one in the place but the regulars. We learned from Sheila that Trina was a crossing guard in Mill Valley; Barbie worked at an adult "theater"; Adolph was homeless; Billy lived in Hunter's Point and sang in a church choir; Freddy played in as many different bands as possible to keep himself off drugs; Treefrog was drinking himself to death; Bobby Spiro had his hands full just keeping it all together.

While Ralph closed his eyes and listened to the music, I sat beside him in the shadows, next to my new friend Sheila, snapping my fingers, rocking my shoulders, nodding my head to the beat.

One week, I dropped Ralph off at the bar and went to a meeting with my boss. Sheila kept Ralph company. When I came back, she whispered into my ear, "Your husband says you went to a meeting. What meeting? We all go to meetings here." She smiled knowingly.

It took me a moment to realize she was referring to a Twelve Step program.

"Yes, Sheila," I answered, "I did go to a meeting, but . . ."

Before I could finish, Sheila put her arms around me and gave me a weak hug. "It's all right, sweetheart," she said kindly, "you're one of us and we love you. Get me another cup of coffee, will ya? I've got to hit the loo."

Chapter 46

CAR PROBLEMS

JERRY WENT TO A card game one night. Afterwards, when he came outside, he found the van tires slashed. He took a bus home.

"How could that happen?" I asked. It was the same question I had asked when the Honda's windows were smashed with a hammer by someone Jerry said he had beaten at dominoes. I was starting to repeat myself.

"Baby, it was a card game. Ain't you ever been to a card game?"

I had, actually, spent most of my formative years underneath card tables, eating mixed nuts and martini onions while my mother and her sisters and my grandmother played championship bridge at the country club.

"Why yes, as a matter of fact, I've been to plenty of card games," I answered.

"Well then, you should know. Shit happens when you play cards."

∽◦∾

We drove down to Big O Tires in the Honda. I waited while Jerry went inside. Through the window, I watched him talking to a muscular black man behind the counter. Together, they rolled a set of tires out the front door and heaved them inside the trunk.

"Baby, you got any money on you?" Jerry leaned his head inside the passenger's side window. "This dude'll sell me these tires directly, for less than what they sell for, but I gotta give him cash."

I looked inside my purse. "I've got sixty dollars."

"Baby, give me fifty."

I gave Jerry the money. He gave it to the man standing nearby. Jerry shook his hand and slapped him on the back.

"I don't suppose you got a receipt, did you?" I asked as we pulled away.

"Girl, don't ya know nothin'?"

I didn't bother answering.

A few days later, as I was getting into the car with Jerry, I noticed the words SNOW TIRES in raised letters across the rubber.

"Now there's something we don't need," I sneered.

"Want me to go back and get different tires?" Jerry asked.

"No, thank you."

∽o∾

I volunteered to pick up chairs and deliver them to the gym for a charity event. I pulled up to the side door of a church and started loading the chairs inside the van. As I cleared newspapers, empty soda cans, and dirty paper towels out of the way, I noticed two brown paper bags in the side pocket of the backseat captain's chair. I pulled out the paper bags and found two large, empty thirty-two-ounce bottles of St. Ides malt liquor.

Damn it, I thought. Jerry has gone too far. It's bad enough the van smells like cigarettes, and that before the radio was stolen, it was always tuned to a rap station. I constantly worried about smashed windows, slashed tires, and an empty gas tank. The week before, I'd found a bobby pin on the passenger seat. A bobby pin! What was that doing in my car?

I finished loading the chairs, went to the gym, unloaded them, and drove home. I took the empty bottles in the brown paper sacks up to Jerry's room and confronted him while he lay in bed.

"What are these doing in the van, Jerry?"

Jerry squinted at the paper bags. He slowly raised himself onto his elbows. He looked inside the bags.

"Goddamn, baby, I am sorry. Those belong to Road Dog. I told that motherfucker not to leave that shit in the van. Girl, I am sorry. It won't happen again."

"Road Dog? You've got somebody by the name of Road Dog sitting in the back seat of the van? Who the hell is sitting in the front seat with you?"

"Guinea Hen," answered Jerry.

∽o∾

About once a week, my supervisor, Tam, would offer me advice on living my life.

When I told him about our bird, he said, "You know Suzy, you might want to find out the nutritional value of a macaw and also a recipe on how to cook one. I've heard they're very tasty."

I ignored him.

When I told him about Jerry's gambling habits, he said, "You know, you might want to look into schools that teach people how to gamble and win. Maybe you could invest in Jerry."

Wow, I thought, finally a suggestion that might work. But when I mentioned it to Jerry, he said, "Baby, I always win. It's only later that I lose."

Chapter 47

A Visit to the DMV

ONE NIGHT, WHILE I was driving over the Bay Bridge, the license plate on the back of the van flew off. It wasn't until the next morning that I noticed it was gone. I realized then why the car behind me had swerved so erratically, and why so many others had honked their horns. I could picture the plate spinning wildly in the air and disappearing into the gloom.

Its flight might have caused a major disaster on the Bay Bridge. It could have been responsible for a severe pileup in which innocent people were killed. I might have spent half the night standing alone on the side of the bridge, shivering in the cold, wondering whether to jump.

I called the Bay Bridge authorities to see if they had found the plate, but they hadn't. I called the Department of Motor Vehicles. They told me I had to come in and complete the paperwork for new plates.

At the DMV, I filled out three pages of forms, front and back. I explained why I could walk but needed disabled plates. I explained why I was there and Ralph wasn't.

The lady behind the desk told me that I was in the wrong line. I looked up above me at the sign and read it for the twenty-fifth time.

"It says 'Disabled license plates'. That's why I'm here."

"I know what it says," she answered, irritably, "but you are not disabled."

"I know I'm not disabled," I answered. "My husband is."

"But you can't stand in the disabled plate line because you are not disabled."

"But I need disabled plates." My voice rose several octaves.

"But you are not disabled yourself," said the DMV official officially. "So you need to stand over there and hand in the paperwork. This line is for disabled people only."

I looked at the line she pointed to with her perfectly mani-cured finger. It snaked around the inside of the building and out the far door.

"Let me speak to your supervisor," I whispered.

The clerk and her supervisor let me stew while they dis-cussed the situation in private, several feet away. They looked at a computer screen and at the paperwork. They stared at another computer screen and pulled a new set of papers from a file drawer.

The supervisor waddled over to the counter. "I'm sorry, ma'am, but you are in the wrong line. We can't serve you here. Your husband will have to come in and complete these forms."

"But he can't write," I sputtered. "He can't move his legs, he can't move his hands, he can't even take a shit on his own." The people behind me stepped back.

"I understand, but you still can't stand in this line," said the supervisor gently. "And by the way," she added. "We need you to complete these two forms as well and bring us a notary-stamped proof of power of attorney. So stand over there in that other line, or I can make an appointment for you to come back early next week." The supervisor peered at me over her enormous glasses, then shot a look at a security guard who was standing nearby. He took a step in my direction.

I made an appointment for early the following week. I went home and slammed a few things around. I took a couple of extra Zoloft tablets, drank a generic beer, pulled all the shades down, and went to bed. It was four o'clock in the afternoon.

✺

I drove around with no back license plate for three months, and I didn't get in trouble with the police.

I dared people to look at me wrong when I pulled the van, with Ralph in it, into various illegal parking spots. I made left turns when the signs said not to. I made right turns when I knew I was breaking the law. I ran stop signs, yield signs, yellow and red lights. I drove over the speed limit on residential streets. I drove under the speed limit on freeways. I did whatever I felt like and was never stopped.

But whenever Jerry drove the van, it was a different story. He was detained by the Oakland police for making a left turn across San Pablo Avenue at a spot where you couldn't turn left. He was stopped for not coming to a complete halt on 56th Street. He was lectured for going too fast on 53rd, and for not having lights on at dusk. He was ticketed for not having a license plate on the back of the van.

One day, Jerry stopped the van in the middle of Dover Street to speak with a neighborhood kid. A police car drove up behind him and followed him into our driveway. They asked him to step out of the car, turn around, put his hands above his head, and lean on the van. They patted him down and rifled through the glove compartment. They didn't find whatever it was they were looking for, and so they let him go. I watched the confrontation from the kitchen window.

"Jerry," I said when he came inside the house, "that wasn't fair."

"Baby," he answered, "ain't no big deal. Ain't nothin' new. Ain't nothin' I can't handle. Life ain't fair. Ain't you learned that yet, girl? You sure should know that by now."

Chapter 48

Throwing Out the Past

I HAD TO CLEAN out the garage. It was out of control. Jerry, Harka, and Mrs. Scott had been saving cans and bottles for nearly six months. I told them they had to remove them from the garage immediately.

"If they aren't gone by sundown," I warned, "I'm going to give your collection away to the shopping cart guys."

"You can't do that," said Jerry incredulously. "We've been savin' those cans for a long time. They're worth twenty, forty dollars by now."

"Sorry," I said without sympathy. "They have to go."

Jerry and Harka loaded the big green bags of beer cans and wine bottles into our van. Jerry gunned the engine and put the van into reverse. They both looked out the window at me with disgust as the van backed down the driveway. I knew whatever profits they might make would be gone before nightfall.

I went into the small garage. It was dark and cool and cluttered. It had once been Ralph's workshop and storage area, and he had kept it neat and well-organized. Now things were in disarray.

His drafting table was a confusion of wood chips, pieces of

cut wire, rulers, pencils without points, and scraps of paper. Everyone who had helped us with making minor modifications to our home had left something behind. Juan, the handyman, had forgotten to file the drawings for the built-in computer table and bookshelves that now took the place of a couch in our living room. Richard, Ralph's brother, had neglected to put away a roll of contact paper and a bag of brass tacks, leftovers from modifying the portable commode.

Sheets of colored glass and the design for a stained-glass lamp Ralph had planned to make crowded one corner. Calculations and sketches in his big, bold hand sat as he had left them only days prior to his accident. Three pairs of roller blades, two tents, a camp stove, snowshoes, and backpacks of various sizes were scattered on dusty shelves and hanging on hooks. A pedestal sink purchased long ago, when we had plans to remodel the upstairs bathroom, was now filled with bolts and screws, sockets and tangled orange and black jumper cables. Eight different pairs of skis—downhill, telemark, cross country, and skate—stood along one wall. A spare tire, old license plates, hubcaps, and the sheepskin seat covers from the Honda were piled in a dark nook. The Italian racing bike Ralph was riding when he had his accident was propped in the shadows, crunched almost beyond recognition. The bloody helmet and the bicycling clothes the Emergency Room personnel had cut off his mangled body were stuffed into a brown paper grocery bag, hidden from view in the musty darkness. I always knew they were there.

It all had to go. There were too many reminders of our previous life. Months ago, I had sold Ralph's old climbing gear to a friend. I'd felt guilty, but it had had to go. Ralph would never notice. He and his wheelchair couldn't squeeze into the garage.

In the middle of the chaos, Jerry had thrown a box full of plastic flowers and Christmas lights from his dead mother's home. Beside the cardboard carton lay a bag full of rusty tools, cans of oil, dead car batteries, and an old red cooler. Inside the cooler were waterlogged, decaying *Playboy* magazines, dog-eared and covered in black mold. I threw them in the trash along with capless pens, bent nails, buckets of prehistoric paint, notecards with Ralph's handwriting.

While I was rummaging through the mess, Jerry and Harka returned from their trip to the recycling center. Jerry peered into the black hole, hands on his hips, surveying the confusion.

"Where's my momma's flowers and Christmas lights? Where's my old red cooler?" he asked, sounding suspicious.

"The one filled with *Playboy* magazines?"

"That's right. You didn't throw 'em away, did you?"

"No way," I answered. "They must be in here somewhere. But what, may I ask, do you want with old plastic flowers, Christmas lights, and rotting *Playboy* magazines?" I tried to make my voice sound casual.

"SENT-I-MENT-AL VAL-UE, darlin'. They be all I have left of my momma. And those *Playboys* be worth a fortune some day."

But other people's sentimentality was something I didn't have time for, an emotional cost I couldn't afford. It brought me too close to the precipice I'd been backing away from since the accident, a place that still had the power to suck the breath out of me even when I took plenty of antidepressant pills.

"Well," I said, in a high-pitched and unsteady voice, "they must be in here somewhere . . . unless Richard took them by mistake. That could've happened, you know. And Ralph's bloody clothes, the ones they tore off him at the hospital, they could still be in here, too. I wouldn't poke around too much if I were you, Jerry. No telling what you might find. No telling what might happen. No telling how you might react. No telling how many dead, old, moldy disgusting thoughts you might dredge up."

Chapter 49

GROWING

OUR GARDEN USED TO be one of the few places where Ralph and I worked well together as a team. Ralph bought the plants and planned where they should go; I planted them. I would have liked to have more say, but going along with him was easier than arguing—plus, we both enjoyed the results. We received lots of compliments, and the garden flourished.

After the accident, our friends were forced to tear up part of the garden to put in the wheelchair ramp. My friend Annie had tried to dig up as many plants as possible and transplant them into the backyard while the construction was going on. Some things made it; some didn't. The Mexican sage survived, but the sweet jasmine died. She couldn't find the tulip bulbs, the zinnias were too young to move, and the Iceland poppies were almost dead anyway.

It didn't matter. Once the construction was done, I didn't have the time or the energy to work in the yard, and Ralph seemed unaware that we had ever had a garden. He could no longer get into the backyard; even the front area was difficult for him to see from his permanent perch in his wheelchair.

For two years, the garden lay neglected. Mrs. Scott made a

half-hearted attempt to grow greens and tomatoes, but she was too big and too old to bend over and take care of them.

Then one spring, the urge hit me. I started weeding, pruning, planting, and killing snails. I bought bulbs, seeds, little tender plants, and anything that was on sale in the Pac n' Save gardening section. I got a composter from the county, a rake from Goodwill, and encouragement from everyone.

Things started growing. Plants I didn't know were there sprouted: strawberries, blackberries, and raspberries; lettuces of all kinds; radishes, carrots, squashes, and beets. But what got everybody's attention, what stopped the neighbors in their tracks, and had the homeless bottle collectors in awe, were my sunflowers: four of them, right in a row.

I grew them from seed. If you squinted your eyes, it looked like Kansas or a scene from "Jack and the Beanstalk." Ralph went outside in his wheelchair and had to lean back to see the tops. The sunflowers were magnificent. Mrs. Scott, Jerry, and Harka thought I should charge the neighbors to come and look at them.

Early one morning, I went outside to water and pamper my babies. I looked up at the sunflowers. Someone had stolen the third one on the left. The head was sheared straight off. The thief had left a trail of delicate yellow petals that went down the driveway and into the street. There, the track abruptly ended.

Jerry lumbered down from his bedroom and surveyed the damage. He said, in his know-it-all, seen-it-all, street-wise, been-there-done-that voice of authority, "I knew it would happen." Then he went back to bed.

Mrs. Scott limped over, shook her large head, and said, "Lord, have mercy, you just can't trust nobody these days." After that, she had to sit down.

Harka looked confused. "Suzy, how could this happen in America?"

Ralph didn't stop watching the Giants on TV, but he said, "Goddammit."

When I told my daddy back east what had happened, he shouted into the telephone, "Those son of a bitches."

I tried to be reasonable. "It could have been squirrels, or pigeons, or that wild green parrot that lives in Mr. Fontenot's backyard."

"I don't think so," answered Mr. Fontenot, thoughtfully, from his porch next door.

And my mother, who doesn't smoke or curse or talk loud or gamble or think a bad thing about anybody, said, "Bastards. They ought to put people like that in jail."

Chapter 50

INTRUDERS

I WAS IN THE kitchen cooking dinner one night when Jerry tiptoed into the room and whispered, "Suzy, don't move. There's a dude watching you at the window." He picked up a large knife that had been lying on the counter and guided me into the next room where Ralph was watching television with the shades drawn.

"There's a dude out there looking in the window, watching Suzy," Jerry explained to Ralph, "and there's another guy, I think, out back casing the house." Jerry walked slowly to the back door and checked to make sure it was locked. He then checked the front door. I stood frozen in the dining room. Ralph, of course, was permanently frozen.

"What should we do?" whispered Ralph.

"Stay where you are," Jerry answered. "I'm going upstairs to look out the window."

I moved toward Ralph and put my hand on his shoulder. No words were spoken between us, but the unthinkable was communicated. What if these men came into the house and robbed and abused us? How could I protect Ralph from intruders? How could I get him out of the house? What if the earth shook him out of bed or flames leapt around his still body? We both knew the answer.

Jerry came downstairs, smiling.

"What is it?" I asked.

"Nothing," he answered. "It's not two guys. It's one guy and he's getting a blow job from a woman. He's right in front of the kitchen window, and she's on her knees."

"Omigod," I shouted. "That's disgusting! Get 'em outta here! Get a hose and spray 'em! Throw something on them!"

Jerry went into the kitchen and picked up the best available weapon on the lower shelf of the butcher-block table—a can of creamed corn. He lumbered back upstairs with his weaponry, but by the time he got there, they were gone. He came downstairs, opened the front door, and scanned the street. There was a man on the corner smoking a cigarette.

"Well," said Jerry, closing the door, "that didn't last too long." He went back upstairs to rest. Ralph continued to watch TV.

I went into the kitchen to finish cooking dinner. "Goddam it," I hissed as I violently stirred the boiling pasta and banged the lid back onto the pot. I didn't have just Ralph, Harka, Jerry, and Mrs. Scott to worry about anymore. Now I had perverts in the garden and natural disasters to think about, too.

Chapter 51

FAMILY PICTURES

In their rooms, Harka and Jerry have photographs of their mothers. Sometimes I peek.

Harka's photo is tacked to the wall above his bed. The picture was taken outdoors. His mother's slender body is clad in a purple-and-orange sari. A multicolored turban is wrapped carefully around her forehead. Her high cheekbones are framed by dangling gold earrings. Through her nostrils is a thick gold ring. Her brown, callused hands grasp the top of a wooden stick. Behind her, rice paddies step up a hillside. She looks directly at the camera, unsmiling.

Jerry's mother's photograph is black-and-white and wrinkled, as if it's been through the laundry or stuffed in the back pocket of too-tight Levi's for too long. It sits on a pile of miscellaneous junk on top of a minirefrigerator Jerry uses as a nightstand. In the snapshot, a young woman sits on a stool, leaning against a bar, a row of bottles in the background. Her bare legs are crossed underneath a tight, knee-length skirt. On her feet are stiletto-heeled shoes with small holes cut out in front for her toes to peep through. She holds a cigarette in one hand, and she is laughing. Smoke curls toward the top of the photo. Her chin tilts up, her eyes are half-closed, her full lips are spread, sensuously. She looks as if she's having a very good time.

A recent Polaroid of my mother sits on my own dresser. Palm trees sway in the background as she stands sturdily in spiked golf shoes, clad in navy blue Bermuda shorts and a matching crocodile-emblemed shirt. A white visor perches low on her forehead, a number-six iron is in her firm grip. She smiles warmly at the camera.

Another photograph rests on top of one of Ralph's television sets. It depicts our newly formed family: Jerry, Harka, and me, squeezed closely together behind Ralph in his wheelchair. Mrs. Scott sits regally beside him. Ralph smiles at the camera. His face is obscured by the mouth stick, door opener, and control rod that are connected to his wheelchair to assist him in the simplest of chores. Mrs. Scott is dressed in a shapeless African print dress. She wears a sequined knit cap and clasps her hands together as if praying. On every finger is an enormous gold ring, set with a sparkling stone.

To Ralph's left, Harka barely smiles into the camera. He is dressed nattily in a suit jacket, wide-collared shirt, and a red, white, and blue tie depicting the Stars and Stripes. His straight black hair, cropped short, frames his high cheekbones. His olive-colored skin appears dark next to Ralph's almost translucent face.

On Ralph's right, Jerry looms large and robust, his ebony skin and ample features contrasting with Ralph's grayness. He smiles broadly under a bushy black mustache. A small gold stud in his right ear twinkles. He is dressed in a T-shirt that advertises beer. A thick, muscular arm reaches between the wheelchair headrest and Ralph's shoulders. Looking closely, one can just barely discern the faded tattoo of a naked lady embellishing his forearm.

Between Jerry and Harka, I look small and gaunt. My smile seems forced. I am dressed in a wrinkled shirt and my shoulders sag as if under a burden. We are jammed together tightly so that the photographer can capture all of us in the lens of his camera. No one is touching Ralph. His wheelchair is in the way.

Chapter 52

THE PLAYER

JERRY TALKS ABOUT HIS daddy with great respect. In the 1930s, he drove back and forth from New Orleans to San Francisco, running drugs, gambling, and pimping. When he met Jerry's mother, he settled down. But soon after, he went back to his old life.

Jerry was born in Louisiana while his father was on the West Coast. His mother got a divorce, moved to San Francisco, found work in a shipyard during the war, and sent Jerry to live with relatives. After the war, she was hired as a domestic by a white family in Fresno.

Jerry lived in Southern California's Imperial Valley on a sharecropper farm that his skinny Uncle Ulysses managed. He stayed there for years, until he was caught messing with the daughter of a Mexican farmhand. His uncle sent him back to San Francisco with his momma, who was now taking care of elderly people in the city.

Jerry grew up on the streets. He learned to drag race cars. He saw his daddy a few times, impregnated Rosemary, a junior high school girl, when he was 18, married her, went to jail for pandering, came out of the clink and hacked around. He dabbled in pimping and drugs, just like his daddy before him.

He talks about his father as if he were a hero. It took me a while to realize that in Jerry's whole life, he had only seen his daddy a dozen times. He died of a heroin overdose before he was fifty.

Jerry keeps a faded, tattered black-and-white photograph of his old man on his bureau. The picture depicts a handsome, slim, light-skinned black man, dressed in a suit and tie with a hat cocked jauntily over one eye. He is leaning on a shiny, new Cadillac and he has his arm around the waist of a slim young woman dressed in a tight skirt, low-cut blouse, and heels. They both hold cigarettes between their fingers and are smiling directly at the camera. There is no doubt that Jerry's daddy was a player.

Chapter 53

HORACE AND MIZ LUCY

ONCE, ON THE WAY home from taking the van to be fixed, Jerry took me on a side trip to East Oakland, a place I'd only been via the freeways that crisscross above and around it. We went up Fruitvale Avenue and made so many right and left turns, I had no idea where we were. Finally, Jerry made a wide U-turn and pulled in front of a small, gray stucco house. A chain-link fence surrounded a tiny yard. Several pink camellia bushes bloomed in front of a neat bungalow.

"That's where my Auntie Armilda used to live," Jerry said softly, his eyes becoming moist. "That's where I began my attendant career, takin' care of Auntie Armilda. She'd be almost one hundred now, if she was still alive."

"Jerry, how long did you live here?" I asked.

"Four or five years. Then I moved back in with Momma and took care of her till she died. Then I tried that pimpin' game again. Then I moved over to North Oakland and took care of Angus."

"Jerry, I don't understand how you could go from taking care of two old ladies to pimping and then taking care of quads. It's such a strange path."

"Baby, it ain't strange. I told you before. Pimpin' is all about takin' care of people. I took care of those women like they were my sisters. I tried to get them off drugs and into the square life. They didn't do nothin' they didn't wanna do. I just protected them from the streets. Shit, ain't no way you gonna understand. Hey, look over there. It's Miz Lucy."

Across the street, a small black woman had come out onto her wooden porch to water a scrawny camellia bush. Jerry rolled down the window and shouted to her. "Miz Lucy, how are you? It's me, Jerry. It's been a long time."

The woman looked up and squinted. "Why, Jerry, it *is* you! Where you been? We ain't seen you in so long. Come over here, boy, and let me see you."

Jerry turned and said to me, "I want you to meet these folks. Miz Lucy was a friend of my auntie and a friend to everyone else, too. Come on."

We got out of the car and crossed the street. Jerry kept his hand on the small of my back and firmly steered me toward Miz Lucy. Whenever we went anywhere in public, he always held me this way. It was a gesture I was unfamiliar with but liked. In the twelve years I had spent with an upright Ralph, he had never placed his hand on my back and guided me anywhere.

Jerry introduced me to Miz Lucy and then began a conversation with her that left me struggling to keep up. Miz Lucy invited us into her house so that we could visit with Horace, her husband.

We walked through the living room, dining room, and kitchen, into a dark room where a television shed the only light. A thin man in satiny pajamas slumped inside a rocker that was too big for him.

"Horace," Lucy shouted, "look who's come to see you. It's Jerry, Miz Armilda's nephew. You remember Jerry, don't you?"

The man's yellow eyes looked up into Jerry's face. "Why, yes, Jerry," he said in a soft, raspy voice. "How are you? Who's this with you? Hello, honey."

"Hello," I said and offered my hand, which he grasped weakly and shook.

"Horace spends a lotta time watchin' TV, specially those ball games," explained Lucy. "Can't get enough of those games."

"Is that right, Horace? You like them games?" asked Jerry.

"Sure do," the little man replied. His eyes traveled back to the television set and glazed over. Horace was no longer a part of our conversation.

Lucy looked at Jerry. "Horace and I been married fifty years. Fifty years. Ain't that somethin'?"

"No kiddin'? Good Lord, Miz Lucy, now that is somethin'." Jerry shook his head in disbelief.

"Fifty years," clucked Miss Lucy. "Ten children, twenty-five grandchildren. Don't even know how many great-grandchildren."

"Miz Lucy, we got to go." Jerry grasped Miz Lucy's small, wrinkled hands. "But it sure is good to see ya. You're lookin' fine as always."

"Jerry, you come back anytime. We're always glad to see you. Suzy, Jerry here, he was awful good to his auntie. He took care of her like she was his own momma. He was good to her, that's for sure."

Jerry put his large, warm hand on the small of my back and guided me across the street. He opened the door for me and helped me inside. Then he went around the other side, got into the car himself, gunned the engine and made a screeching U-turn that burned rubber. I grabbed hold of the armrest and braced myself for disaster as I always did when I was in the car with Jerry.

Chapter 54

Fourth of July

WE HAD NO PLANS for the Fourth of July.

I tried not to think about the past: the Independence Day Ralph and I had spent hiking in the Canadian Rockies; the year we stood on top of Mount Rainier together; the time we bicycled in the south of France; the July we kayaked around Angel Island in San Francisco Bay. For the past two years, Ralph and I hadn't gone anywhere on the Fourth of July. And the next day's holiday would be no different. We weren't invited to a barbecue, a fireworks display, a parade, or a picnic. It would be just Ralph and me alone in the house, like every holiday and weekend since his accident.

By now, I should have been used to it, but I wasn't.

I fought traffic all the way home from work. Minivans packed with kids, coolers, and beach chairs whizzed by me. SUVs loaded down with bicycles, kayaks, Windsurfers, and Boogie boards slammed on brakes. Cool-looking couples in sleek convertibles gave me no notice as they zigzagged in and out of traffic, pulling campers, boats, and three-wheelers. Everyone else was going somewhere fun, and I was heading home to North Oakland.

∾o∾

"What should we do tomorrow?" I asked Ralph as I came into the dining room. He sat frozen in his wheelchair and stared at the television set. In the next room, another TV was on, tuned to a different station. Canned laughter emanated from one set and gunfire from the other.

"I don't know, " he mumbled. "What day is it?"

"It's Independence Day. I don't have to go to work."

"Maybe you can take me to the video store," my husband answered, not taking his eyes off the set. "I want to see what's new there."

"Okay," I said softly, but inside I was raging. When would we stop going to the neighborhood video store for entertainment? When would the television sets be turned off? When would I finally get to do what I wanted to do? When would someone invite us somewhere and give us an alternative to Blockbuster, Channel 2, and ESPN?

I went into the kitchen to make dinner.

∾o∾

After I had fed Ralph, put away the leftovers, and washed the dishes, I rejoined him in the dining room. He continued to gaze at the TV. I flopped down on the couch in the living room and watched the other set.

The telephone rang, interrupting a rerun of M*A*S*H on one station and the Giants versus the Cubs on the other.

"Is Jerry there?" a squeaky female voice asked.

"No, he's out," I answered. "Can I take a message?"

"This is Rosemary. Tell him I'm having a barbecue tomorrow and I'd like him to come."

"Okay, does he have your number?"

"Oh, yeah, he has it. Tell him to call me."

I recognized the name. Rosemary was the woman Jerry had married forty-three years ago. She was the ex-wife who had rediscovered Jerry after Ralph began reporting his wages to the IRS. Because of Rosemary and two little girls who were now middle-aged women, we were paying the San Francisco district attorney's office $150 a month for child support payments dating back to 1954. It was one of the methods we used to keep Jerry at home, in our employment, and out of jail.

"Rosemary called," I yelled to Jerry from my nest on the couch when I heard him come in later that night.

"Oh yeah? What she want?" He headed straight into the living room and pulled the covers off Ralph's hospital bed in the corner.

"She wants to invite you to a barbecue tomorrow. She wants you to call. Jerry, can Ralph and I come with you? It's the Fourth of July and no one has invited us anywhere."

Jerry rolled his eyes at me as he started the long process of putting Ralph to bed. "Lemme think about it," he answered.

"Jerry, I want to meet your family." I whined.

"You really want to meet them?" He was unbuttoning my husband's shirt, blocking Ralph's view of the television.

"Yes, I do. Ralph wants to meet them too, don't you, Ralph?"

"Who?" Ralph asked. "What are you talking about?"

"Jerry's been invited to Rosemary's house tomorrow for a barbecue. I want him to take us along."

"Who's Rosemary?"

"You know who Rosemary is. She's Jerry's ex-wife, the one we pay child support to in San Francisco."

"I thought we paid someone in Oakland." Ralph sounded confused.

"That's Nina," I explained. "Nina is the one in Oakland who has Celeste. Rosemary is the one with the two daughters about my age."

Jerry had Ralph in bed by now. He disconnected the catheter from the bag around Ralph's leg and hooked it to a large jar on the floor. Tomorrow morning, the jar would be filled with Ralph's amber urine.

"Jerry was married to Rosemary a long time ago," I continued, "back when he was just a kid. Isn't that right, Jerry? Isn't Rosemary the one you split up with after San Quentin?"

"Girl, how am I supposed to know? That's ancient history. I can't remember what happened to me forty, fifty years ago." Jerry slid a long strand of dental floss between Ralph's teeth.

"The district attorney's office and Rosemary seem to remember it pretty well," I pointed out.

"I can't keep up," mumbled Ralph when the flossing was done. Then he was quiet. Jerry was brushing his teeth.

"Okay," said Jerry, looking down into Ralph's mouth as the electric toothbrush whirred. "I'll call her in the mornin'."

"Call her now, please?"

Jerry placed sleeping pills on Ralph's tongue and held a glass of water to his lips. Then he covered him with a thick blanket and pulled up the rails on the hospital bed.

"Good night, Ralph. See ya in the morning." He hit the overhead light.

I tiptoed over to the bed and bent down toward Ralph's pale face. It almost glowed in the dark.

"Good night, sweetheart," I whispered, kissing him on his cool cheek. "I love you."

"Okay," he whispered thickly. He was not far from sleep.

I followed Jerry upstairs.

"Call her now," I pleaded to his back.

"Who?"

"Rosemary!"

"Oh yeah, lemme find her number."

I waited while he looked for the crumpled scrap of paper on which he kept her telephone number. I handed him the portable phone and watched him as he dialed and listened for someone to answer.

"Rosemary, that you? How are you, baby? Yeah, boy. Got your message. Say, I'm fixin' to bring the family with me tomorrow, if that's okay with you. Yeah? All right. What time? Want us to bring somethin'? You sure? Okay. See ya then. Bye."

Jerry turned off the telephone and handed it back to me. "Rosemary says four o'clock. You really want to do this?"

"Oh, yeah. We're family, right?"

"Yeah, girl, you heard me. I'm bringin' the family."

I could hardly wait until the next day to tell Ralph the good news.

☙◦❧

In the morning, Jerry dressed and shaved Ralph and placed him in his wheelchair. I made potato salad, deviled eggs, and a big pound cake. I packed beer, soda, and wine in a cooler. I wanted to make a good impression on Jerry's kin.

The barbecue was in Hunter's Point, an area of San Francisco I had never visited, but a place I had often read about in the paper. I knew from the eleven o'clock news that Hunter's Point was riddled with guns, dope, and prostitution and populated by out-of-work black men. Hunter's Point had section 8 housing, welfare mothers, and high school graduates who couldn't read. Before I even got there, I thought I knew what Hunter's Point was like.

But Rosemary's house, set on a steep hill, was neat and tidy and full of friends and family. People moved sofas and chairs so that Ralph could squeeze into the living room. A barbecue grill took up the entire backyard.

Wings, ribs, links, burgers, hot dogs, and pork chops sizzled on the grill, billowing smoke into the sky. Bowls of dips and chips, jars of condiments, plates of cornbread and cupcakes and pies crowded a picnic table and jammed the dining room sideboard. I helped myself to a plate of food and chatted with an enormous elderly woman who had known Jerry since he was just a "twinkle in his daddy's eye."

Jerry introduced me to J. D., Eel, and Puddin', old friends from the neighborhood. They wheeled Ralph up to a folding table and dealt him a hand of cards. Jerry juggled a plate of food for himself and Ralph and held Ralph's cards at the same time. Together they ate and played, winning some rounds and losing others

A kaleidoscope of color, texture, and noise swirled around us. Jerry's cousin Renae told me about Aunt Armilda and Jerry's mother, Lilian. Jerry's daughter, Loretta, discussed her office job and the classes she was taking at San Francisco State University.

Our hostess, Rosemary, forced additional paper plates of food upon us and introduced me to Jerry's ex-stepchildren, aunts, cousins, and second cousins. His two grandchildren stood back, sneaking shy looks at their grandfather. Jamal was big and lanky, with long black braids cascading down his back, colorful beads around his neck, and plaid boxer shorts peeking above his sagging Levi's. I could see a sixteen-year-old, tattooless version of Jerry in Jamal's wide, sexy smile. Taking after her mother and grandmother, Mahisha was small and outgoing. I learned from her proud father that she was a freshman at U.C. Berkeley, hoping to go to law school.

A deep belly laugh snared my attention. I looked across the room. It was Ralph. His chin was tilted toward the ceiling and he was grinning from ear to ear. He was obviously having a good time. I caught Jerry's eye. He winked at me. I gave him the thumbs-up sign and helped myself to more macaroni salad.

Later, as we climbed into the van to leave, everyone gathered around us, shaking Jerry's hand, patting Ralph on the back, giving me hugs. Puddin' said to come back anytime. J. D. agreed, adding that he always liked to play cards with people he could beat.

"My God!" I said to Jerry and Ralph, clutching the armrests as we roared down the hill in front of Rosemary's house and sped onto the freeway, the big van rocking with the turns, Jerry's foot, heavy as always, on the accelerator. "Jerry, that was wonderful! Thank you so much."

"Yes, it was," shouted Ralph from the back of the van where he sat strapped down, unmoving and isolated.

"Oh yeah?" Jerry answered, switching lanes and blowing the horn at slower vehicles. "Bet you didn't know I had such good-lookin' babies, did you? Didn't know an old San Quentin graduate like me could have a grandkid at Berkeley studying law, did ya?"

"No, I didn't know that. I learned a lot about you and your family today."

"Our family," corrected Jerry.

"Yes, you're right. Our family."

I looked out the window at the sailboats skimming across San Francisco Bay. We hadn't backpacked eighteen miles or slogged up Mount Shasta in a blizzard, but we had made it over the bridge and into a new neighborhood and a new family. We had come a long way. I hoped Rosemary would invite us back again next year.

Chapter 55

TULARE

Jerry announced that he had to attend a funeral in Tulare. A great-aunt had died. His daughter Celeste and her mother, Nina, had made arrangements to rent a car, drive down to Tulare, spend the night, and come back the next day. He was packing.

All day, he seemed sad and agitated. He took a long bath, shaved his head, trimmed his goatee, powdered himself down and oiled himself up, clipped his nose hairs and his ear hairs, dragged out a suit bag, a shoulder bag, and a little brown-and-tan suitcase.

He packed carefully, folding things just so, then put on a pair of tight, neat jeans and a polyester sweater that strained against his broad chest. He took out his gold hoop earring. In its place he put an enormous gold J. He hung a gold chain around his neck and snapped a gold bracelet around his thick wrist. Then he carried his bags out onto the porch and waited.

I watched out the window as a shiny red compact car pulled up to the curb and two large women emerged. They were dressed in fancy outfits and high heels. Their black hair cascaded down their backs in thin braids. They opened the trunk. Jerry put his luggage inside and slammed it shut. The two

women held a door open for him. He squeezed himself into
the rear seat. The women got into the front bucket seats and
drove away.

I had expected Jerry to jump behind the steering wheel,
move the seat back, adjust the mirrors, and change the radio station. But it was obvious who was in charge, and it sure wasn't
Jerry.

Chapter 56

RAISING CHILDREN

My FRIEND LINDA BROUGHT her two little boys, Will and Ryan, to our house. They ran wild, jumping on the furniture, running up and down the wheelchair ramp, bouncing on the bed in the back room.

Linda did nothing to stop them. She laughed at their antics and, by doing so, encouraged them to misbehave more.

Mrs. Scott left the house muttering under her breath, "Those damn children ain't got no manners and their momma ain't got no sense." She stayed away, waiting at the front door of her apartment, until she saw Linda pack the boys into her minivan and head for home. Then Mrs. Scott came back and gave Ralph and me a lecture on how children should be raised. "They be my kids, I'd slap their behinds all the way into next week," she said, shaking her head in disgust.

Jerry came downstairs. "I heard that," he shouted. "Knock them into Christmas or whatever comes first." He went into the kitchen, opened the refrigerator door, peered inside, and let out a deep sigh of disappointment. He scooped himself a big bowl of vanilla ice cream. As he passed through the living room, he added, "Those damn kids need some discipline." Then he went back upstairs to eat ice cream and play solitaire.

Later that night, I crawled into bed next to Jerry. He gave me another lecture.

"Those kids need to get their butts whipped. My momma knew how to raise children. She didn't take shit from anybody. No sirree, Momma Carter raised me right. And when I lived down on the ranch with my Uncle Ulysses and my Aunt Priscilla, they didn't take no shit neither.

"I remember one time, me and my friend Salathiel went into Uncle Ulysses' cantaloupe patch. He had a big old patch of melons. And we cracked open every goddamn one of those melons and ate the hearts outta them and I got that cantaloupe juice runnin' down my face and my Uncle Ulysses, he hit me upside the head and said, 'Goddam boy, what ails ya?' Then Aunt Priscilla cut herself a switch outta tree and put my head between her legs and smacked the tar outta my butt and you can bet I never did that again. No sirree, my people knew how to raise me."

I stared at Jerry. Will and Ryan would probably graduate from high school and go to Harvard or Princeton or both, earn degrees in medicine and law, and move somewhere near a country club and raise more children just like themselves.

Jerry had spent his life pimping, selling drugs, scheming, stealing, making babies, and running from the law. But somewhere along the way Aunt Priscilla, Uncle Ulysses, and Momma Carter must have knocked some sense into him, because he knew how to take care of Ralph and me.

Chapter 57

MRS. COOPER'S FUNERAL

THE TELEPHONE RANG AT 6:30 A.M. I answered it groggily and hoped whoever was on the other end wouldn't hear Jerry snoring.

"Suzy Parker, it's Momma Scott."

I could tell she was crying.

"What's wrong?"

"Mrs. Cooper died, baby. The funeral's today at eleven o'clock. Be here by ten-thirty to pick me up. We can't be late." Mrs. Scott hung up the telephone.

As usual, there was no discussion as to who would take her to the funeral, just as there was never any debate as to who would carry her to Pac n' Save or to the dentist. We were friends. Friends with cars took friends without transportation to places they needed to go. And in return, Mrs. Scott gave me her undying love and devotion, whether I wanted it or not.

At 10:30 A.M., I blew the horn in front of Mrs. Scott's duplex. She came out, dressed in a calf-length, pale yellow chiffon dress. A horizontal ruffle around the hem rose to a peak halfway up her enormous backside. She teetered down her stoop in white high heels. Her yellow beret almost matched her dress. A rhinestone pin appeared to be keeping the cap attached to her head.

"Mrs. Scott, you look nice. Are you feeling any better?"

"Do I?" Mrs. Scott asked, fluttering her eyes. "Why thank you, darlin'. But I just feel so bad 'bout my cousin, Mrs. Cooper. She was ninety-three years old, Suzy Parker. That's old, baby, but not that old." She began to sob.

Through her tears, she gave directions to the funeral home. I dropped her off and found a parking spot around back. She waited for me in the foyer, and together we walked down the aisle to the front pew.

"This is for family only," a woman in the second pew whispered to us as we took seats up front.

"We're family," Mrs. Scott replied. She sat down, then grabbed my arm, and yanked me down with her. The pew rocked backward and then forward, and then was still as Mrs. Scott settled in.

"Mrs. Scott," I murmured into her ear. "I'm not family."

"You stay where you are, child. You're family to me and I'm family to Mrs. Cooper. We're all family here."

But soon a large group of people, mostly women and children dressed in black, filed up the aisle to the front pew. They stared at Mrs. Scott and me. "This is the family," someone hissed loudly from the pew behind us. "You've got to move."

I slid right along the bench and out the other end, leaving Mrs. Scott in the front pew. I tiptoed down the side aisle to the last seat in the chapel. Mrs. Scott stayed where she was, and I watched the others crawl over and around her.

When the music and singing began, I could hear Mrs. Scott's voice above all the others. When the minister began to speak, Mrs. Scott nodded her head and shouted in agreement with him, "Oh, yeah, praise be the Lord. That's right."

I hadn't known Mrs. Cooper very well, but I knew her enough to know that she and Mrs. Scott had been friends for over forty years. They had both moved from East Texas to Oakland during World War II. They had both raised families in North Oakland and they both had a slew of grandchildren and great-grandchildren. Whether they had actually been related by blood was not as clear. I gathered they were cousins from somewhere far back along the family tree. Not that it mattered. As Mrs. Scott had said, we were all family here.

When the service was over, Mrs. Scott walked down the aisle slowly. I met her at the last pew.

"Come on, baby doll, let's go home," she whispered to me, her eyes bloodshot, her cheeks streaked with tears.

"Yes, Momma Scott," I answered quietly. "I'll go get the car."

Chapter 58

LOVE

ONE NIGHT IN BED, I whispered to my snoring companion, "Jerry, I hate to tell you this. I don't want to scare you, but I have to say it. I love you."

The snoring abruptly stopped. A long silence ensued, then Jerry scooped me up in his big arms and said "Me too you, baby."

∽○∾

Another night, Jerry rolled over and whispered into my ear, "Baby, I love you. You're beautiful and kind and generous and sweet. I love just about every thing about you. I need you. I depend on you. I love you. It scares me."

I didn't roll over, but I said, "Me too you."

Later, at 5 A.M., I poked Jerry on the shoulder and asked, "How much do you think you might love me?"

"One, two, three, four, five, " he grunted, half asleep.

"What's that mean?"

"One, two, three, four, five," he repeated.

"What?"

He slowly rolled over and looked at me. "That's what I used

to tell my momma when she asked me that same question. One, two, three, four, five. Girl, I used to think five was the top of the world!"

∽∘∾

At 2:35 A.M. the following night, the telephone rang. Jerry woke up and answered it after the sixth ring. I could hear a woman shouting, "Why did you leave? Why don't you come over now? What's wrong with you, anyhow?"

Jerry mumbled apologies between the shouts, hung up the phone, turned on his side, and began to snore almost immediately.

I tapped him on the shoulder. "Excuse me," I said. "What was that all about?"

"Huh?"

"Who was that?"

"Wha'?"

"That phone call, who was it?"

"That phone call?"

"Yes, that woman asking you to come over. What was that about?"

"Oh, that. Nothin'."

"Nothing?"

"Nothin'."

But I wouldn't let him go to sleep. I poked and prodded and patted and fondled and licked and sucked until he had no choice but to make love to me.

When it was over and he was puffing on a cigarette, I asked again about the phone call and he said again it was "nothin'."

And I, who could never leave anything alone, left it alone,

because I was too scared to really want to know who had been on the other end of the phone line and what she may have wanted from Jerry.

∽०∾

Jan, the fastest climber in the world, had become my friend.

Tall and thin, with long blond hair, piercing blue eyes, and abdominal muscles to die for, he was a Marlboro man in Indonesia, a part-time stunt man in Hollywood, a nude calendar model, and the fastest person to climb Yosemite's famed El Capitan and Half Dome.

He was thirty-three years old, lived in the suburbs with his mother, and worked out every day at the gym when he wasn't hustling to get his name and picture on a PowerBar or Gatorade advertisement.

Jan thought carefully about everything before he spoke. He was the only fan of Ayn Rand I had met since eighth grade. His sponsors kept him up to date in the latest sunglasses, the coolest sandals, the baddest T-shirts. When I'd pop out with Jan for something to eat, his "coolness" rubbed off on me and I became a totally rad person myself, not at all like a forty-four-year-old woman in charge of lost and found at a climbing gym.

Sometimes Jan would stop by our house and visit with Ralph and his coolness rubbed off on him as well.

Jan would tap Ralph on the breastbone and say "Ralph, do you feel that?" Then he'd run his fist gently down Ralph's stomach. "Do you feel this? This? This? Do you ever feel hungry? Can you feel your stomach growl? Can't you move that finger even a little?"

Ralph would laugh and answer his questions. It was always a

refreshing visit, and after Jan would leave, we would feel good for knowing such a cool guy.

Jan was the only person in two years to invite us to his house for dinner. When we told him that we probably couldn't come because it was likely we couldn't get up the steps into his mother's house and maneuver around her furniture, Jan said "Never say never. I am getting you into the house."

So we went over to Moraga. Only fifteen minutes away, but it felt like halfway around the world. Jan had laid out boards on all the steps up to the house, and he pushed and squeezed Ralph into the front door and through the kitchen to the dining room. And there we had a lovely dinner, made by Jan, and afterward we watched slides of him climbing in Malaysia and Thailand, and Ralph fell asleep.

When we arrived home, Ralph declared that it was the best evening out that he had spent in a long while. I said good night to my husband and left him watching Jay Leno. I went upstairs.

In the dimly lit bedroom, Jerry sat on the bed playing solitaire, naked, except for a pair of black socks.

"Hi," I said.

"Don't talk to me, girl," he said, staring at the cards.

"Why not?" I asked.

" 'Cause you been out with that skinny blond motherfucker."

∾o∾

A few days later, Ralph looked up at me from his bed, his eyes bright and shining. With the joy and enthusiasm most of us reserve for winning the lottery or giving birth to a healthy child, he said, "Jerry is going to give me a bath!"

I ran the water and opened all the doors, so that once Jerry gathered Ralph in his arms it would be a straight shot into the bathroom.

Jerry picked up my helpless husband. Ralph's pale white body lay limp and stark against Jerry's broad brown chest. Ralph's steel blue eyes looked into Jerry's warm green ones with trust and devotion. Jerry carried him down the hallway, into the tiny bathroom, and gently set him into the tub. Then he bathed Ralph as a mother would bathe her infant—with care and gentleness and love.

∽∘∾

Not long after, Jerry and I were awakened by Ralph's moans. We could hear him through the intercom. At first the moans were low, but gradually they became more and more loud and sorrowful. Soon they became a chilling wail we could hear without the aid of the intercom.

Jerry rolled out of bed, slid into a pair of old sweat pants lying on the floor, and went downstairs to investigate. I could hear the scrape of furniture moving, the opening and slamming of drawers, and the heavy, quick steps of Jerry in action. It wasn't his usual shuffle.

I got up and started down the steps. I ran into Jerry on the landing, racing up the stairs.

"He's sick," he shouted. "I need towels." He pushed past me.

I went into Ralph's bedroom. He had vomited all over the bed and on to the floor. I turned around and gagged. The stench was unbearable.

Jerry returned, his arms full of towels. He lumbered past me and said, "Suzy, leave the room. I'll take care of this."

I walked unsteadily through the dining room and the kitchen. I unlocked the back door and leaned over the deck railing, feeling clammy and sick. I could hear Jerry talking low to Ralph, changing sheets, gathering up bed linens, starting the washing machine. I stood still and listened to the sounds of North Oakland at two in the morning.

Jerry came outside and stood behind me. He leaned against me hard and put his arms around my waist. "Come on back in. Everything is fine. Let's go to bed."

I let him lead me through the now-darkened downstairs room, up the stairs, and into our room. Jerry closed the door, turned on the overhead light, covered me with a sheet and blanket. He opened his bedside refrigerator and pulled out a carton of ice cream. He helped himself to a big bowl and began to eat.

When he finished the ice cream, he ate a small bag of corn chips. Then he munched on some salami and cheese.

"Jerry, how can you do that?" I whispered, flat on my back, staring up at the ceiling. "How can you eat after everything you've just seen and done with Ralph?"

"Baby, that's my job. Ain't no big deal. Life goes on. C'est la vie."

He stood up and turned off the lights. He took off his sweat pants, rolled into bed, slowly undressed me and made love to me, gently, sweetly, kindly.

∽o∾

Another night, I was awakened by a shouting match. I looked at the bedstand clock. It was 2:35 A.M. I heard Jerry yell, "Who do you think I am, man? You think I got all night? Shit, you think all I do is lay in bed waitin' for you to go to bed? Shit, I'm not waiting around no more!"

I jumped out of bed, threw on the clothes I had left on the floor, and dashed downstairs. I met Jerry on the bottom step.

"What's going on?" I asked.

"Shit," he answered. "Ralph can't think of nobody but himself. I'm sick of this!" I could tell by his sharp tone and stiff posture he was furious. He didn't look at me as he passed by.

I went into the living room to find Ralph staring at his computer.

"Fuck Jerry," he screamed. "He can't wait five fucking minutes while I finish here. Fuck him!"

Jerry banged back down the steps. "What you say, man? Why'd you call me down here, if you ain't ready? It's two-thirty in the morning, Ralph. I've been here since midnight. Midnight! Two-and-a-half hours later and you still ain't ready. Shi-it!" He stomped back up the steps.

Ralph began to cry. "Calm down," I whispered. "I'll put you to bed, sweetheart. It's okay." I held Ralph's head in my hands as he sobbed. It was the only part of his body I could get my arms around while he was strapped in the wheelchair.

I heard doors slam upstairs and then Jerry's feet thumping down the stairs again.

"I'm sorry, Ralph," he said softly. "I lost my cool. Suzy, go to bed. I'll take care of Ralph."

But I didn't go to bed until I was sure they were both calm and that Jerry wouldn't physically hurt Ralph. I understood Jerry's frustration. Waiting around for Ralph was no picnic. But I could never comprehend Ralph's situation. It was too enormous. And except for the occasional outbursts of shouts, Neanderthal-like raving, and snot-running sobs, he never let me know what he was feeling.

Thirty minutes later, Jerry crawled into bed. He pulled his pants off and rolled over on top of me. With no pretense at foreplay, he pushed himself between my legs. He moved against me harder and harder and harder, until, with a loud grunt, he came and then collapsed on top of me. Two hundred and thirty pounds of him was stifling, but I lay quietly underneath him, trying hard to find comfort in his now inert, slick body.

There wasn't any doubt in my mind that Jerry had taken his frustrations with Ralph out on me. But I didn't feel used. I was glad it was me he wanted to make love to and not Ralph he wanted to hurt.

Chapter 59

BABIES

San Francisco's Carnaval parade took place near the gym where I worked. When there was a free moment, I went out on the street to explore.

I pushed past tattooed Hispanic teenage girls in hot pants, hoop earrings, and black lipstick. I slipped past automobiles that danced to music by remote control. I bought some tacos and cruised up and down the street, sticky salsa dripping between my fingers. I looked at all the booths. I watched the people swirling around me, couples hand in hand, mothers pushing baby carriages, fathers holding toddlers. I wanted to hold or push one of those babies myself.

When I returned to work, I glanced at the brochures I had gathered from the booths outside. I had kept only two: a flyer on home composting and a brochure on how to adopt a baby.

Something was going on in my head, but I was afraid of what it was. I no longer wanted to curl up in Mrs. Scott's lap. I wanted to hold and cuddle a baby.

◈

I was alone in the office at the gym when I had the miscarriage. There was blood everywhere on the floor. I didn't know it was coming. I didn't even know I was pregnant. But it had happened before, so when it happened this time, I knew what it was.

I walked unsteadily into the ladies' room and stuffed paper towels down my pants. I went back into the office and wiped up the floor as best I could. I called Kaiser and made an emergency appointment. I was shaky and sweating profusely as I went to my car and drove over the Bay Bridge. But the worst had passed, and by the time I arrived at the doctor's office, it was over. I went home with the same instructions I had received in the past: rest, drink plenty of liquids, call the ER if hemorrhaging or pain occurs.

At home, Ralph was asleep in his wheelchair. He wasn't expecting me for some hours. I tiptoed past him and went upstairs. I found Jerry in bed. I crawled in beside him and told him the news.

"How'd that happen, baby?" He put his arms around me.

"I don't know," I whispered, still in shock. "How do you think it happened?"

"Your body can't handle no little black baby, can it girl?"

"Guess not," I answered, barely breathing.

"Woulda been a fine-lookin' baby."

"Yes, and smart, too."

"Just as well. Be pretty hard to explain."

"Yes."

"Woulda been a looker, though."

"Yes, would have been a looker."

"And a player."

"That too."

"Coulda changed the world."

"Yes," I answered. I held on to Jerry and wept.

∽◦∾

The miscarriage was not the first, nor the second, nor even the third that I had had.

Several years before Ralph's accident, I had had a miscarriage that sent me to the hospital for days of tests and monitoring and finally a D&C. Months later, I had another, and then another. Each happened within days of home tests that showed I was pregnant.

Rather than supporting Jerry's theory, the doctors had told me I had a deficiency in certain hormones that affected my ability to carry a fetus. Before Ralph's accident, I had been taking hormone pills and fertility drugs, but nothing had worked.

I had taken the drugs halfheartedly; Ralph had been unsupportive, which had made me ambivalent. But, as time wore on after Ralph's accident, I knew I wanted something more than a life spent taking care of Ralph. Jerry satisfied some needs, but I was worried that time was running out for me to become a mother.

I was still adjusting to the fact that I would never have my own biological children, and hoping that some day I could adopt a child. But now we didn't have much money, and I had to work. I wondered if any adoption agency would find our home fit for raising children.

I kept all these thoughts in my head and I didn't share them with anyone. They were too painful.

I didn't have any idea what I was going to do. But slowly, I realized I was creating a family with the materials at hand: Ralph, Jerry, Harka, Lolita, and Mrs. Scott. It wasn't the family I had hoped for. But we were a family, I was sure.

Chapter 60

GRADUATION

MY BROTHER JOHN FINALLY graduated from college and was accepted to the University of California School of Veterinary Sciences in Davis. It was one of the happiest days of our lives. His road to graduation had been a long, arduous, and some-times painful journey from junior high school through several two- and four-year colleges. Then, right when John was making real progress, Ralph had his accident. John was stuck at home fielding telephone calls while I was at the hospital. In the days that followed, he was busy caring for me. He flunked some of his exams and never bothered to take others. But, finally, at the age of twenty-nine, he'd attained his goal. I have to admit, there were times when our family doubted he would make it, except for one member—Mrs. Scott.

"We're goin' to Davis," Mrs. Scott would shout, pounding her fists on our dining room table. "And don't let anybody tell you no different, WE ARE GOIN' TO DAVIS." She chanted this phrase almost every day throughout John's last two years at Hayward State.

She wore a black chiffon floor-length evening gown with a rhinestone bodice to graduation. She was her usual glitter, twinkles, and stars, and she caused quite a sensation when she swished into the gymnasium at Hayward. Of the hundreds of people there, all celebrating with the class of 1996, Mrs. Scott was by far the most dramatically dressed. By the end of graduation, everyone knew who she was: John Parker's other mother, the one who had got him into veterinary school.

At a post-graduation party, she spontaneously fronted a punk rock band and sang a gospel tune dedicated to John. Later in the evening, after dinner, she sang another, this one a cappella. You could hear a pin drop in the restaurant. People cried. When she finished, strangers came by our table to congratulate John and hug Mrs. Scott.

"Our son did it!" Mrs. Scott boomed across the table at my mother. "He did it! He's going to be a doctor now, oh yeah!"

"Yes," said my mother, beaming with pride. "And he couldn't have done it without you, Mrs. Scott. You prayed him through school, and I will always be grateful."

"Thank the Lord above for that," corrected Mrs. Scott. "I got nothin' to do with it." Then she turned to John and commanded, "Come over here, sweet baby, and give both your mommas a kiss."

And that's what my brother did, because he believed, as we all did, that in conjunction with a lot of blood, sweat, and tears, long hours of study, and years of hard work, it was Mrs. Scott's faith in him that had pushed him through college and on to veterinary school. There are all kinds of faith in this world. Some of it is religious, some of it is blind, but faith in another human being, faith in his potential and in the power of positive possibilities counts for plenty. I've seen it work. I've been a witness.

Chapter 61

OVERDOSE

ALL IN ALL, IT had been a bad week. On Monday we'd learned that Ralph's checking account was overdrawn. On Tuesday, we found out my checking account was overdrawn. On Wednesday, the credit card companies said we owed them more than $300 in interest. On Thursday, the property tax bill arrived. On Friday, Ralph took himself out to Piedmont Avenue and wound up three miles from his destination. He ran out of power and had to stop a pedestrian and request help. The Good Samaritan knocked on the door of a nearby house and asked to use a telephone. He called the number Ralph gave him and Jerry came to the rescue.

On Saturday, our friends Paul and Natalie came over to cook dinner and take us to a movie. While Paul was helping Ralph into the van, Ralph went backward rather than forward and fell off the end of the lift. He went down hard, about three feet, to the concrete driveway. Paul yelled for Natalie and me.

I yelled for Jerry. We ran outside to find Ralph coherent, tipped over on the ground with his wheels spinning. His massive, pillow-encased headrest had saved his life. It took all four of us to turn him upright. We decided not to go to the movies and went inside and had a few drinks instead.

Ralph's getting lost and falling off the lift seemed to be part of a pattern. He was taking so many drugs, I worried they might be affecting his mind. He ingested massive doses of Valium, baclofen, and Dantrium for spasms. He took trazodone to sleep, ciprofloxacin to fight infections, and Minipress to keep his blood pressure low. He took vitamin C, vitamin E, and vitamin B complex. He popped cranberry pills to clean his urinary tract system and stool softeners to loosen his bowel movements.

He experimented with the timing of each dosage, and he argued with the neurologist over milligrams and centigrams. He approached his medications with the scientific training and fervor he had learned as a postgraduate at Cal Tech. When the neurologist told him that drinking beer while taking Valium, baclofen, and Dantrium might kill him, he immediately stopped drinking.

Some days, he was listless, drowsy, and confused; other days, he was more alert. In either case, he almost always dozed in the late afternoon for a few hours. Often, he didn't follow conversations or understand questions he was asked. He rewatched videos he had already seen. I had to shake him to keep him awake during films.

On Sunday, his speech was slow and slurred. His head trembled slightly. He said it was time we got the neighbor's dog pruned. I thought he'd finally lost it.

On Monday, I called his neurologist, his primary care doctor, and his physiologist. I left voice-mail messages for everyone. No one called back, so I called again the next morning. Dr. Denton returned my call. "It sounds like he's taken an overdose. What is he taking?"

This was the kind of question that always made me ballistic. Dr. Denton was the one who had prescribed Ralph's Valium.

Didn't he have a computer that could tell him exactly what Ralph was ingesting?

I pulled bottle after bottle of Ralph's pills off his bureau. I shouted their names into the speaker phone as I threw them on to Ralph's bed.

"Listen, Mrs. Hager," Dr. Denton interrupted me. "Calm down, please. It's Dr. Church who prescribes the baclofen. I think that's the problem. Call him."

I hung up and looked at the bottles. Dr. Church had indeed prescribed the baclofen. Dr. Herman ordered the trazodone; Dr. Steiner wrote out numerous prescriptions for Dantrium; Dr. Mason prescribed ciprofloxacin. I wondered if any of them knew what the other was doing.

The next day, Ralph insisted I take him to the video store, the ice cream parlor, the bookstore, and the coffee roasters. When I refused to make all four stops, he came up with a new itinerary. Instead of going to the video store, he would take himself the four blocks from the ice cream parlor to the Oriental rug merchants. I followed along behind him, reluctantly.

At the rug store, Ralph discussed the pros and cons of several pieces with the salesman before deciding on a small square of Oriental rug for eight hundred dollars. I walked out of the shop in disgust when we started to argue about money in front of the staff.

He had to have lost his mind. He knew we didn't have eight hundred dollars. He knew we didn't have fifty dollars. I debated leaving him at the store, but knew that he couldn't get home by himself. In silence, I put him into the van and resolved to pack my bags and get out of his life before our only alternative was robbing a bank.

When we arrived home, there was a message on the

machine from Dr. Church. He said Ralph should reduce the baclofen dosage by one and have an MRI immediately, because things did not sound good. Ralph could have had a stroke. He could have overdosed on one of his prescription drugs. The cumulative affect of the baclofen and the Valium might be causing the slurred speech. And, just like anyone else, Ralph was susceptible to brain tumors, cancer, heart disease, and ulcers.

But before I could make an appointment for the MRI, Dr. Denton called and said not to have it done. At this point, he advised, it was best not to expose Ralph to undue discomfort unless absolutely necessary. Then Dr. Denton told us he had no idea Ralph was taking 500 milligrams of baclofen a day.

I went crazy. "Who the fuck is in charge here?" I shouted into the phone.

But I knew it was a rhetorical question because it appeared that Ralph and I were in charge. And we had no idea what we were doing.

Dr. Denton said to reduce the baclofen to three, the Valium down to one, and to call him on Monday. If Ralph's situation had not improved by then, he would have a look at him.

It was Wednesday afternoon. We had four full days to wait it out.

∽○∾

We returned the rug. Ralph had to think about it long and hard, but eventually he chose me over the small square of Oriental tapestry. I wasn't sure I was pleased by his decision.

I did not go to work. Ralph seemed listless and disoriented, and I thought it would be prudent for me to stay close.

Thursday came and we had plans to go to a movie and dinner. But at the movies Ralph made funny noises. He shouted incomprehensible words at the screen. Something was terribly wrong.

After the movie ended he asked where we were and insisted that we go home. When we returned home, he didn't recognize our living room. I asked him to recite our telephone number. He couldn't. I asked him to tell me his social security number. He couldn't.

Jerry came home, and together we put Ralph to bed. That night, Ralph made animal-like howling sounds. In the morning, he could not speak. His face was bright purple and twisted in a horrifying grimace. His mouth was open wide as though he were screaming, but no noise came out.

I called the paramedics.

Ralph was rushed to the Emergency Room and, after seven hours of poking, probing, testing, and administering more drugs, his condition was diagnosed as acute withdrawal from baclofen and Valium, seizures, low blood platelets, a urinary tract infection, a temperature of 101 degrees, and congestive heart failure.

Chapter 62

NEXT DOOR

IN THE SPACE NEXT to Ralph in the Emergency Room was an elderly woman who couldn't hear very well. Doctors and nurses were shouting at her. I overheard everything that was being said through the thin cotton curtain that separated her bed from Ralph's.

Her name was Viola Smith. She had no relatives, except for a sister in Colorado. She didn't know her sister's phone number or address, and it wasn't clear that she knew her sister's name. The doctor asked her how old she was. She said eighty-three. He asked her who was president. She hesitated and guessed Eisenhower. He asked her what year it was. She answered 1972. He asked her how long she had been lying on the floor of her apartment. She didn't know.

"We're going to clean you up," shouted the doctor. "It's not good to lie in poop. You know that, don't you? You can't lie in poop or you will get sores. Do you know, Mrs. Smith, how long you have had diarrhea?"

"For six months," she replied in a tired voice. "And I haven't eaten in a week. Can I have something to eat?"

"Not yet," answered the doctor, and he left the room.

About thirty minutes later, a nurse came in to see Mrs. Smith.

"Mrs. Smith," she hollered, "we are going to clean you up."

"I can't hear you. What?" whimpered Mrs. Smith.

"We're going to clean you up!"

"Can I have something to eat?" Mrs. Smith pleaded. "I haven't eaten in two weeks."

"Not yet," answered the nurse, and she left the room.

Another forty-five minutes went by. A new nurse and doctor and new orderlies were now on shift.

"Mrs. Smith," someone said, "we're going to clean you up. You can't lie in feces. You'll get sores."

"What?" croaked Mrs. Smith.

But no one answered her. To no one in the room, Mrs. Smith begged, "Can I have something to eat? I am so hungry. I haven't eaten in three weeks."

Chapter 63

SHARING THE GOOD AND THE BAD

In the ICU, Ralph was attached to a zillion machines with lights going up and down and wavy lines running horizontally across the screens. Something dripped into a vein in his hand and something else was being pumped up his nose. A tube snaked out of his penis, but that wasn't unusual.

I gathered from the nurses that they had filled him with all the drugs we had taken away from him, and more. In addition to baclofen, Valium, trazodone, and Dantrium, he was now getting dilantin, a strong antiseizure drug. The seizures had stopped, but Ralph still couldn't talk.

He tracked me with his eyes as I came around to his bedside.

"Ralph, I love you." I leaned over the cold metal railing and planted a kiss on his cool forehead.

As I pulled away, I noticed the faintest trace of a smile cross his phlegm-covered lips, underneath the tubes that went into his nose.

დოფ

They kept telling us that Ralph was going to be moved to another room, but it didn't happen until nine o'clock that night. It wasn't until then that I remembered Ralph had not had a bowel movement in four days. Jesus, I thought, I really am in charge here. Ralph could die from backed-up shit, and I'd be the only one who knew what was wrong with him.

There were more tests and more confusion. Ralph slept most of the next day and mumbled incoherently when he opened his eyes. But most of the time, his eyes remained closed or rolled back into his head.

I ate big cartons of Chinese food and stared at my unconscious husband. I thought about the past, something I usually tried to avoid. Ralph's eyes hadn't always been dull and cloudy and hooded like snake's eyes. His eyes were once bright blue and intense, his body strong and vibrant. He'd peered discerningly at motors, electrical switches, cookbooks, menus, atlases, and backcountry ski maps. He possessed a library full of how-to books and manuals: Sunset's Maintaining a Bonsai Collection; Where to Collect Pre-Columbian Art; You Too Can Run a Sub-Four Marathon; Building a Snow Cave in a Blizzard; DOS for Dummies; Making Pasta at Home. He even wrote a book. It was full of numbers: tables he had developed years ago with his fellow Ph.D. classmates at Cal Tech. But now this book sat on a dusty shelf surrounded by old physics textbooks. It was never a big seller.

There was a time when Ralph had stayed awake at parties and weddings. He was often the first to arrive and the last to leave, after the keg was drained and the coffee served. He never watched television or went to the movies. He read the morning paper from cover to cover, a large cup of hot strong coffee in his right hand, NPR on in the background.

Later that night in the hospital, Ralph woke up. He was able to speak. He saw things I could not see as he stared at the blank television screen above his head. Hairy spiders and purple butterflies crawled and flew down from the ceiling and up from the floor. They hovered around his head and landed on his nose. A huge green thing perched on his chest, its powdery striped wings opening and closing slowly.

"They aren't scary," Ralph said, laughing for the first time in days. "They're friendly and soft. Look," he shouted, turning away from me, "here comes another one!"

I wanted to see it, but I couldn't. I wanted to share something fun with my husband, but it was impossible.

∽◦∾

The following morning, a woman came into the room and identified herself as a wound specialist. She wanted to see the rash that had developed between Ralph's legs. I pulled back the covers. She put on rubber gloves and felt around Ralph's groin area. She clicked her tongue a few times.

"Do you always have a foley catheter inside your husband?"

"No, sometimes we do intermittent catheterization. But the condoms pop off, so the attendants and I thought this was easier and cleaner."

"You should catheterize your husband every three to four hours."

I stared at her. "I can't do that."

"Why not?" she asked.

"It's not humanly possible. The home nurses told me two years ago twice a day is enough. Anything else is too much to ask of anyone."

"You said you have help. Have the attendants do it."

"But I don't have unlimited funds," I answered. "The attendants aren't paid to work all day."

"Well, just think about it."

She took off her rubber gloves, threw them into the waste basket, and left the room.

Asshole, I whispered.

Ralph woke up and said, "That woman is full of shit," which was the only lucid thing he had said in three days. Then he fell back to sleep.

Chapter 64

The Folks Back Home

Jerry and Harka hadn't worked since Ralph left for the hospital on Friday.

"Jerry, are you enjoying your vacation?" I asked when I came home Monday night and found him lying in bed.

"Hell, yes. First vacation in two years."

"What have you been doing all day?"

"Sleep! Til two-thirty. Then I get up and eat and hit the streets."

I crawled under the sheets with him. "Don't go out tonight, Jerry. I need you here to take care of me."

"Okay, baby," he answered as he stroked the top of my head with one hand and with the other used the remote to change the television's channels.

∽o∾

Mrs. Scott called me at seven-thirty the next morning. "What are you doin', sweetheart?" she asked.

"I'm getting ready to go down to the hospital," I answered as I balanced the telephone on my shoulder and reached for the car keys.

"Child, you got a life to live. You can't be takin' care of that husband of yours night and day. Ralph is a very sick man, but you got a life, too. Now listen, Suze, you get dressed and put on some lipstick and go to work. The hospital people will take care of Ralph. You need to get out and go, girl."

"Mrs. Scott, I can't do that right now. I've got to go to the hospital. Please don't yell at me."

"I'm not hollerin' at you, child. I just don't have my teeth in, that's all. All I'm sayin' is that you got to take care of Suzy Parker first. That's all."

⚬⚬⚬

"I'm leaving now. Good-bye." I leaned over and kissed Jerry on the forehead.

"Okay, baby. But wait, ain't you forgettin' somethin'?" he mumbled.

"What?"

"I need some money."

"Oh, of course, how silly of me."

Some patterns don't change, even in a crisis. I found Jerry's consistency oddly comforting.

⚬⚬⚬

Late that night, when I came home from the hospital, I found a message from Mrs. Scott on the answering machine: "Hello, darlin'. It's Momma Scott callin' you to tell you I love you and I think very dear of you and I'm only concerned that you take care of yourself. I wasn't hollerin' and scoldin' you, my dear child, because I love you too much to scold you. And I want you to take care of yourself, sweetheart.

"Today is November the 12th, nineteen hundred and ninety

six. And if I can help you by tellin' you to slow down, then that is just what I'm gonna do. Think and analyze what I'm sayin', baby. That's all I'm tryin' to do, darlin'.

"Please understand. Hope so. I love you. Make sure you call me back now, you hear?"

Chapter 65

DANCING WITH QUADRIPLEGIA

AFTER FIVE DAYS IN the hospital, Ralph was allowed to sit in his wheelchair. It took six hospital employees to figure out how to get him into it. Most of their time was spent watching me maneuver him.

Two hours later, at 3 P.M., the entire physical therapy department came into Ralph's room. "Mr. Hager," said the head therapist, "we're going to have to put you back into bed now. This is the only time we will have enough therapists available."

"I don't want to go to bed yet," Ralph replied angrily.

"I'm sorry, Mr. Hager," answered the therapist, "but the nursing staff here can't put you to bed later. They've called us and asked us to put you down, and this is the only time we can do it."

"Jesus Christ," shouted Ralph. "It isn't fair. I don't want to go to bed!" He began to sob.

"Ralph, don't cry," I whispered. "I'll call Jerry and Harka and see if one of them can come later and put you to bed." I asked the physical therapists, "Is it all right if Ralph's attendant and I put him to bed later tonight?"

"Perhaps," answered the head therapist with a shadow of

relief stretching across his tan face. "Let me see if I can get permission from the nursing staff."

After much discussion, it was decided that an attendant and I
could put Ralph to bed as long as one nursing staff member
was present during the transfer. The physical therapists left in a
hurry. I called home and woke Jerry up. He said he'd come over
at 9 P.M.

Jerry arrived, resembling a North Coast logger who's been in
the forest cutting Christmas trees. He wore a plaid flannel shirt,
black jeans, enormous brown work boots, and a nice olive
green car coat with a brown leather collar, all from the lost and
found at the gym.

He looked rather dashing, and I saw that his arrival did not
go unnoticed by the nurses and orderlies on duty. I went out to
the nurses' station and asked if someone could assist Jerry. Four
women volunteered immediately. They all crammed into the
room. "Watch out now," cautioned Jerry. "Stand back, I don't
want any of you pretty ladies to get hurt."

Jerry took off his coat and laid it neatly on a chair. In one
swooping gesture, he bent down, gathered Ralph in his big
arms, and moved him onto the bed. The attending ladies
shrieked and clapped. "Ain't hard," Jerry told them, "but don't
any of you little ladies try it."

Jerry went out to the nurse's station with his admirers. I covered Ralph with sheets and blankets, brushed and flossed his
teeth, adjusted the television set, packed up my belongings,
said good night, turned out the lights, and left the room. Jerry
was leaning on a counter, laughing with the nurses.

"I'm ready to go now," I announced.

"Well, you ladies take care now," Jerry said to his new
friends. "Nice to meet you. Just call me if you need any help
around here."

"Good-bye, Jerry," they squealed in unison. "Come back and see us anytime."

The handsome logger and I drove home.

∽○∾

Seven days later, the doctors said Ralph could go home. Ralph interpreted their announcement to mean right away, when they meant in twenty-four hours. He had a nurse call and tell me to come and get him. But when I arrived with his street clothes, they said he wouldn't be ready until the next morning. I stayed at the hospital all day and finally returned home around 9 P.M. I was exhausted but relieved that Ralph was going to be okay.

Jerry lay in bed, naked.

"Let's go out, " he suggested.

"All right," I answered.

I put on a dress and makeup, stockings and earrings. I painted my lips red and waited for Jerry to get ready. He put on a pair of pants with an elastic waist. Nothing else fit, but he still looked good to me.

We went down to Eli's Mile High Club, a funky, hole-in-the-wall bar on Martin Luther King Jr. Way. The place was rockin', and when Jerry escorted me onto the crowded dance floor, I held on to him as the saxophone wailed, the bass player picked, and the drummer beat out the blues.

Jerry held me casually around the waist. He pushed me backward, then pulled me forward, all the while grinding his groin into my pelvis. I felt like I was at the high school prom with the sexiest boy in the class. It was embarrassing but also thrilling. My spine tingled and my legs felt weak. I let him lead me all over the dance floor, standing on my toes, pushing and rubbing and hanging on with all my might.

I buried my face into Jerry's chest. I was dancing for the

simple joy of it and I was dancing for Ralph, too, because he was coming home. And I was dancing because we had made it through the week and through two years of hell, and somehow I knew we would keep on plugging away. It wasn't the life we had chosen to live together, and it wasn't the life that society expected us to live, but I was glad to be living it.

I held on tighter to Jerry and let him rock me to the music.

Chapter 66

CONFESSION

ONE MORNING, WITHOUT MUCH forethought, I sat down beside Ralph as he lay in bed and said, "Ralph, we never talk about sex."

"I know," he answered, his words slurred from Valium. "There is nothing I can do about it. I'm sorry."

"But don't you wonder what I'm doing about it?" I stroked his cool forehead.

"Yes, sometimes. But I try not to think about it. I'm not sure I want to know."

"Can I tell you?"

"I don't know." His voice sounded small and hesitant.

"I think I'd like to tell you. I think it will actually make you feel better."

"I don't know that it would," he whispered.

"Ralph, sweetheart, it would make me feel better if I told you. Maybe that's selfish of me. But everything in our lives is so mixed up and turned around, sometimes it seems like hardly anything matters anymore. Certain marriage vows don't make sense, do they?"

"No, I guess not."

"Can I tell you?"

"All right."

"I've been sleeping with Jerry."

Ralph's eyes grew wide. "Jerry?" His voice registered disbelief. "Jerry?" he repeated.

"Yes."

Ralph was quiet for a moment. "I thought you might be having an affair with someone at work," he said quietly. "You stay there so late sometimes. But Jerry? I never thought of Jerry. Never!"

"I know, but don't you see, it's actually to our advantage."

"How?"

"I don't long to be somewhere else, with someone else. I come home to you, and him. It's convenient. He takes good care of me. He takes good care of you. It's weird, I know, but it seems to work."

Ralph was silent. His blue eyes stared at me. "I guess so," he said without conviction. "I'm just so sorry this had to happen. I'm so sorry I had this accident and that you have to take care of me. I'm sorry. I'm sorry. I'm sorry." He began to sob.

"It's okay, sweetheart." I kissed him on his forehead. "We're going to be all right, I promise. We're going to pull through this somehow, I'm sure."

"Yes," Ralph answered. "I hope so."

We were both quiet as we stared at one another.

"Suzy." Ralph's voice was hoarse and desperate.

"What?"

"I love you."

"Me too you, Ralph," I answered, stroking his forehead. "Me too you."

Chapter 67

How

How does Ralph get by? How does he cope? What does he think about? What does he feel? Is he sad? Is he depressed? Does he wish he were dead?

People often ask me these questions. They are cautious with their wording. They want to know the answers, but they are also afraid.

"I don't know," I reply. "I know he does not want to be dead. He's made that clear, but how does he get up and face every day? I have no idea. Why don't you ask him yourself?"

You'd think I might have a clue, but I don't. I doubt that I could be as strong as Ralph if the accident had happened to me. I would feel sorry for myself, I'm certain. I would whine and cry and carry on until everyone around me was miserable. They'd want to lock me in a closet and throw away the key.

"He's an optimist," I say. "He's a trained nuclear physicist, a scientist. He is accustomed to dealing with problems that need a mental, not physical, solution. He looks ahead. He does not look back. He thinks about the future, not the past. He uses the scientific method, whatever that is."

And I love him more now in his disabled state, I think, than I did when he could dance with me.

Chapter 68

A Mugging

HARKA WAS MUGGED AT 11 A.M. near the corner of 51st Street and Broadway in Oakland. The police brought him home, slightly hysterical and more than a little paranoid. Although the incident had occurred two miles from our home, Harka became convinced that he had to move. He sat forlornly on our couch and contemplated his future. "Maybe Canada," he said, rubbing his thin neck which his two attackers had attempted to strangle. "I hear it is safer there."

"Yeah," said Jerry as he passed through the living room on his way to get something to eat in the kitchen. "Canada might be safer. But you know, don't you, that you can stand on a corner all day in Canada and ain't nothin' gonna happen." He stared at Harka. "Nothin'," he added with a meaningful look.

"Jerry," I said. "You've never been to Canada. How do you know that?"

Jerry shrugged. "There's a whole lot of things I know that you don't know."

Harka continued to massage his neck. "Maybe I go back to Nepal. It is safe there. America is not so safe and there are people who want to kill me. Why me? I'm nice guy. I do nothing. I not understand."

"I don't understand it either," I said. "I am very sorry this happened to you, but you have to move forward. You must try to get over it."

"Get over it," said Jerry passing back through the living room with a bowl of ice cream.

"Yes," said Ralph from his wheelchair. "You've got to concentrate on the positive and not the negative."

"Why?" asked Harka. "They take my money. I cannot get over."

For weeks Ralph, Mrs. Scott, Jerry, and I attempted to help Harka with his confusion and depression. We cooked his favorite meals. We loaned him the car. Jerry offered to work some of his shifts taking care of Ralph, but Harka remained gloomy and depressed.

"I don't know how long I can stand this," I said to Ralph. "He's driving me nuts. He's making me depressed. Something has to be done."

"Give him time," answered Ralph, who knows about these things. "He'll come around."

"Yeah," added Jerry sagely. "He ain't goin' nowhere. He just needs to chill."

And so we waited. Ralph's electric wheelchair got stuck in high gear and he crashed into furniture throughout the house and broke some things. I bounced a couple of checks and Jerry lost a few card games. We went on with our lives and slowly Harka's attitude improved. He walked around the neighborhood. He bought lottery tickets. He cooked and cleaned and took wonderful care of Ralph. He rooted for the Golden State Warriors and when they lost to everyone, per usual, he didn't get upset.

Then, without warning, Jerry's back went out and his friend

Leo's electricity was turned off. I cooked Jerry his favorite food and sent some leftovers to Leo, who was sitting in his living room in the dark. "Life ain't fair," complained Jerry, as he left for Leo's.

"You'll get over it," I said.

Chapter 69

FINDING TOMMY

Mrs. Scott called me on the telephone early one morning. "Suzy," she bellowed, "come over to my house right now. I got somebody here I want you to meet."

I dropped what I was doing and walked down to her apartment. In her cramped living room was a middle-aged, balding man beaming fondly at Mrs. Scott. "Look here, Suzy Parker, this is my son, Tommy. Tommy, this here is my daughter, Suzy Parker."

I shook his hand. "Glad to meet you," I said.

"Mutual," he answered.

Mrs. Scott continued. "Thirty-eight years ago, Tommy's momma called me and asked me to look out after him. When I got over to her place, she handed me her baby and said, 'I'm goin' out, I'll be back by eleven o'clock.' Eleven o'clock come round and she wasn't back. I took that baby home. In the morning I called the police. They said, 'We'll take him.' I said, 'No you don't. I'll keep him till his momma come home.' Suzy Parker, you know his momma never did come home?! I raised this boy for two years. *Two years!* And when people said, "What's that black lady doin' with that white baby, well, I just ignored them."

"It's true," said Tommy. "I lived with Mrs. Scott until I was adopted by people in Fresno. I've been trying to find her for a long time. We've just gone to get my birth certificate."

Mrs. Scott looked at Tommy. "We've got to tell Montel Williams about this," she said, tears streaming down her face.

"I'll always be grateful to Momma Scott," Tommy whispered, choking on his words. "She saved my life."

"Oh baby!" squealed Mrs. Scott. "Give your old momma a kiss."

Tommy leaned over and placed a big smacker on Mrs. Scott's round cheek. I couldn't help myself. I did the same. And then I kissed Tommy on the top of his smooth bald head, because after all, he was, in some weird way, my brother.

Mrs. Scott sang out, "Children!" She squeezed her eyes shut, stomped one foot on her apartment floor, swayed from side to side and clapped her hands to a beat that was basic and mournful, both ancient and familiar. *"We've got to learn to love one another,"* she sang. *"Oh yeah. We've got to LOVE one another, oh yeah. We've got to . . . we've got to . . . we've got to . . . we've got . . . to learn . . . to love . . . one another . . . oh yeah . . . oh yeah. . . . Amennnnnn."*

Chapter 70

RALPH RAISES HIS VOICE

I DON'T KNOW HOW it happened. One minute, my friend Gina was residing on a failing ostrich ranch in the easternmost corner of Contra Costa County, selling commodities, and living with a man who played softball six days a week. Then, without consulting me, she moved to 18th and Castro in San Francisco and took up with a woman who had ties to the city's poetry scene. Gina quit her job and began arranging adventure travel trips for the rich. She enrolled in belly dancing classes and developed a keen interest in offbeat theater. Despite the differences in our lifestyles, we remained friends.

Gina and Cathy rented a cabin for a week in Inverness. Tucked among the manzanita, poison oak, and eucalyptus, it looked out over the blue waters of Tomales Bay and the brown hills of western Marin. Ralph, Harka, Jerry, Mrs. Scott, and I were delighted when they invited us to their home-away-from-home for a barbecue.

We made our way out to the deck, where an eclectic mix of Gina's past and present friends drank malt liquor, pink ladies, and Queer Beer. A drag queen plucked on a guitar and a woman with a pierced nose beat her bongo drums. Inside the house, pushed into a corner, was an ancient player piano. Box upon box of well-worn song rolls filled the shelves above it. While Gina's softball-playing ex-boyfriend gave a detailed account of his failed ostrich business and Juanita Hairdryer, a performance artist from New York, acted out her latest piece, people gathered around the player piano.

Artie pumped the machine, working up a sweat and cursing under his breath when a roll slipped. He warmed up with *"Daisy, Daisy, give me your answer true,"* and continued with *"I wanna gal just like the gal that married dear old Dad."* Gina's theatrical friends joined in and improvised. They slipped in raunchy lyrics, shouted insults at one another, and argued about what to sing next.

When some of the men began to sing *"I'm a Yankee Doodle Dandy,"* Ralph excused himself from the lecture on the difference between two-toed African ostriches and their three-toed South American relatives and from Juanita Hairdryer's performance of "Alphabet City on Ecstasy." He put his wheelchair in gear with a tilt of his chin, spun his chair around, and headed for the player piano.

Within moments I could hear him harmonizing with the group. *"I want to wake up in the city that never sleeps,"* then moving on to *"Chicago, my kind of town,"* "Oklahoma," "Old Man River," "Nothing Like a Dame," and "I'm Gonna Wash That Man Right Outta My Hair."

Everyone loved Ralph. They egged him on and squeezed in closer, putting their hands around his shoulders and wheelchair. "Sing it, Ralph!" shouted Timothy. "Ohhhhh, baby, hit it," moaned Pablo.

And Ralph did. He sang louder and louder and louder. I could hardly believe he was my husband, so strong was his voice, so clear his words, so joyous his tune. He belted out Rosemary Clooney, Fats Waller, and anything by Rodgers and

Hammerstein with an ease and spontaneity I had not known he possessed. When Artie put in the roll from the musical *Fame*, Ralph let out a ritornello that stopped everyone cold. *"Fame!"* he shouted. *"I'm gonna live forever—I'm gonna learn how to fly . . ."*

The softball-playing ostrich farmer got quiet. Juanita Hairdryer slowed down. Timothy, Cathy, Pablo, and Gina looked as if they might cry. Artie kept pumping and Ralph kept singing. His voice soared out of the little cabin in the woods, floated down to the sleepy village of Inverness, drifted out over the blue-green waters of Tomales Bay, and bounced back to us off the brown hills of Marin, confirming what we now knew and hoped and loved about Ralph: *"Fame! I'm gonna live forever—I'm gonna learn how to fly . . ."*

Chapter 71

IN THE MIDDLE OF THE NIGHT

ONE NIGHT NOT LONG ago, Ralph awoke at 3 A.M. "Help," he shouted weakly through the intercom next to his bed. Upstairs, I heard his cries. "Help," he repeated. "I need help."

Neither Jerry nor Harka were home. Jerry was out on one of his usual covert night runs, and Harka was in Reno. I was home alone with Ralph and the bird. I got up.

"I'm coming," I shouted as I slipped on a T-shirt and hurried downstairs.

Ralph's face glowed white from his hospital bed, lit up by a streetlight outside the front window.

"Stretch my arms," said Ralph. "Take off these covers. I'm hot."

I pulled the blanket and sheet down to his feet. I grabbed one of his limp arms, and supporting it at the elbow, lifted it high over his head. I leaned in close to his face.

"How are you?" I whispered.

"Not good," he answered, his eyes closed. "Maybe this will help."

No words passed between us as I balanced my body against the arm beside his head. I thought about how late it was and how alone we were. I recalled that I was once a person who

liked to rise early and go to bed by 9 P.M. Getting up in the
middle of the night was something I never did, unless it was to
pack for an early morning ski trip to the Sierra. But now getting
up in the middle of the night had become routine.

"Okay," said Ralph, his eyes still closed. "Now do the other
one."

I gently lowered his right arm and placed it beside him. I
stretched across his body and slowly lifted his left arm above
his head, then placed his elbow beside his ear and tried not to
press my weight against his chest.

∽○∾

I used to feel sorry for myself when I had to get up three or
four times in the middle of the night. But time has a way of
making things easier. I've developed a little game that I play
inside my head while I'm trying to make Ralph comfortable.
I think of the other people who are up at two in the morning with me: air traffic controllers, waitresses, the copy guy
at Kinko's, nurses, doctors, firemen, and the police. There are
lonely people in bars, stock boys filling shelves at Safeway, people out on the street with no place to go. While it's the middle
of the night in California, Nasdaq is opening on Wall Street. In
England, it's time for fish and chips; in India, it's the hour for
high tea. Over in Indonesia, millions of people are hustling
about: riding bicycles, waiting for buses, carving small wooden
knick-knacks for tourists. In New Zealand, it's getting near time
to milk the cows, and in Hawaii, it's happy hour. Somewhere
there are mothers breast-feeding children, cooking dinner for
their families, waiting for their loved ones to return safely from
parties, wars, and jails. At this very moment, when I feel the
lowest, there are births and deaths and situations too tragic to
imagine. I am not alone. I'm lucky to be where I am.

❦

"All right," said Ralph. "You can lower my arm now."

I placed it by his side, then pulled the covers up to his chin and tucked them tightly around his neck so that he wouldn't get cold.

"Raise the head of the bed, please."

I went to the foot of the bed, kneeled down, found the crank, and turned it so that the bed rose slightly.

"That's good," said Ralph. "Thank you."

"Sweet dreams," I whispered. I kissed him softly on his cool forehead. "I love you, Ralph. Don't let the bedbugs bite."

I listened for an answer, but he was already asleep. I went upstairs to Jerry's room and waited for him and Harka to return home safely.

Epilogue

AFTER SIX YEARS, WE have adjusted to our situation. It's not perfect, but it seems to work. Ralph fills his days watching sports and movies on television, designing and maintaining his personal website (www./rshager.com), and dabbling in on-line stock market trading. I hope he'll get better at this endeavor soon. He continues to volunteer for the Center For Independent Living. He is currently president of the board and he chairs the program services, executive, personnel, and finance committees. He works very hard, and as in high school, he has perfect attendance at every meeting. The Center for Independent Living is lucky to have him.

We rarely talk about the past. It doesn't work for us to think about our former lives. We don't see many of our old friends because we don't share the same activities. It's just as well. Old memories are painful. We can't go back there, so we don't.

Ralph has never brought up my relationship with Jerry. Sometimes I think he may have forgotten about it, but I'm not sure. He looks only forward, not back or to the side. I am in awe of his strength and fortitude. He is truly an amazing man.

Jerry is still with us, although I have fired him at least a dozen times. But he has not left, because he knows I don't really mean it, he hasn't anywhere else to go, and we are his family. I sleep with him sometimes, but not always. I am not as needy as I used to be. There are some things about Jerry that I will never understand. There are cultural, social, economic, and educational issues that I can't change and lines I can't cross. Because of the differences in the way we were raised and have had to interact in society, I know that he understands me much better than I know him. Sometimes I think he knows me better than I know myself.

Harka has decorated his bed in Martha Stewart knockoffs, his walls with vintage Marilyn Monroe posters, and his ceiling with American flags. His closet is full of new clothes—jackets and shirts, pants, belts and shoes. The centerpiece of his room is a plastic globe that glows in the dark. Press any country and a deep, serious voice will tell you the names of the highest peaks, the most profitable cash crop, and the number of automobiles driven by its populace. Harka is a citizen of the world—a man who delights in the everyday miracles of life on this planet, including those little ones that occur on Dover Street. He has made us thankful for the things that we have, most importantly his friendship and love.

Mrs. Scott has become something of a jet-setter. A year ago she got back together with her old, bad ex-husband Albert. She spends several weeks each month at Albert's home in Reno. The rest of the time she splits between Albert's house on West Avenue and her own apartment on Dover Street. Always independent, she is not ready to give up her own place for any man, and especially not for Albert. I still take her to her doctor's appointments, to Pac n' Save, and to Costco. I listen carefully to her advice, and more often than not, I follow it.

Tommy, Mrs. Scott's adopted son, comes to visit quite often. He has become an integral part of our weird little family

My brother John married a wonderful Japanese woman last August. Mrs. Scott sang at the wedding. Harka, Tommy, Ralph, and I danced together at the reception. Jerry watched from the sidelines. He has never been a big fan of marriage.

We still have Lolita the macaw, but as far as I'm concerned, she's for sale. She will live to be about 103 years old. At that longevity, she is an incredible bargain and long-term investment.

Last Valentine's Day, we acquired another family member. Jerry's youngest daughter, a nine-year-old, arrived on our front steps. "Daddy," she said as she walked in our stained-glass front door.

"Oh my God," whispered Jerry. "Where did you come from?" Harka and Ralph stared in amazement. Lolita let out a frightening squawk. Mrs. Scott shook her head knowingly. Jerry swept the little girl up in his big, strong arms and gave her a bear hug. Jernae now stays with us on the days her mother works. It's always good to have a kid around to keep the adults in line.

As for me, I spend my days writing sarcastic essays for the local paper, driving Ralph to meetings, restaurants, and movies, and just generally trying to hold things together. I have taught Jernae how to ride a bicycle, swim, ice skate, bowl, and count her change when she buys candy at Pac n' Save. I regard these accomplishments as some of my most rewarding experiences.

Friends, relatives, and complete strangers continue to give me advice, but for the most part I ignore them. I've learned that no one can tell another person how to live her life. And I know that as long as I don't hurt anyone, and if I keep an open mind and try to be a generous, tolerant human being, that somehow, someway, we'll keep chugging along. It is not the life Ralph and I planned to have together. It is not the family I had once hoped for. But it is a family of sorts, with all the idiosyncrasies that every family, however traditional or makeshift, might have. We are not without joy or laughter or love. Ralph and I remain optimists. Somehow we'll get by.

Jack and Jill went up the hill
To fetch a pail of water.
Jack fell down
And broke his crown
And Jill came
Tumbling after.

Jill got up
And looked around
To find Jack
Hurt and broken.
She picked him up and
brushed him off
And took him home
To love him.

Author's Note

With the exception of the immediate families of myself and my husband, Ralph, Jerry, Mrs. Scott, and Harka, I have disguised the names and identifying characteristics of the people in this book to protect their privacy.

Portions of this book apeared in different versions in my columns for the *San Francisco Chronicle*, the *Sun Magazine*, the *San Jose Mercury-News*, the *Santa Cruz Sentinel*, the *Washington Post*, the *Chicago Tribune*, *Hope*, ebility.com, the *East Bay Express*, and *Wellspouse* newsletter.

About the Author

SUSAN PARKER lives in Oakland, California, with her husband, Ralph, her friends Harka Bhujel and Jerry Carter, a very large bird named Lolita, and a tiny dog misnamed Whiskers.